DAILY STRENGTH FOR BOYS

BroadStreet KIDS

BroadStreet Publishing Group, LLC.
Savage, Minnesota, USA
Broadstreetpublishing.com

DAILY STRENGTH FOR BOYS

© 2025 by BroadStreet Publishing®

9781424569816
9781424569823 eBook

Devotional entries composed by Natasha Marcellus.

All rights reserved. No part of this publication may be reproduced, distributed, or transmitted in any form or by any means, including photocopying, recording, or other electronic or mechanical methods, without the prior written permission of the publisher, except in the case of brief quotations embodied in critical reviews and certain other noncommercial uses permitted by copyright law.

Scripture quotations marked NIRV are taken from the Holy Bible, New International Reader's Version®, NIrV® Copyright © 1995, 1996, 1998, 2014 by Biblica, Inc.™ Used by permission of Zondervan. All rights reserved worldwide. www.zondervan.com The "NIrV" and "New International Reader's Version" are trademarks registered in the United States Patent and Trademark Office by Biblica, Inc.™ Scripture quotations marked ICB are taken from the International Children's Bible®. Copyright © 1986, 1988, 1999 by Thomas Nelson. Used by permission. All rights reserved. Scripture quotations marked NLT are taken from the Holy Bible, New Living Translation, copyright ©1996, 2004, 2015 by Tyndale House Foundation. Used by permission of Tyndale House Publishers, Carol Stream, Illinois 60188. All rights reserved. Scripture quotations marked NIV are taken from the Holy Bible, New International Version®, NIV®. Copyright © 1973, 1978, 1984, 2011 by Biblica, Inc.™ Used by permission of Zondervan. All rights reserved worldwide. www.zondervan.com. The "NIV" and "New International Version" are trademarks registered in the United States Patent and Trademark Office by Biblica, Inc.™ Scripture quotations marked NCV are taken from the New Century Version®. Copyright © 2005 by Thomas Nelson. Used by permission. All rights reserved.

Typesetting and design by Garborg Design Works | garborgdesign.com
Editorial services by Michelle Winger | literallyprecise.com

Printed in China.

25 26 27 28 29 30 31 7 6 5 4 3 2 1

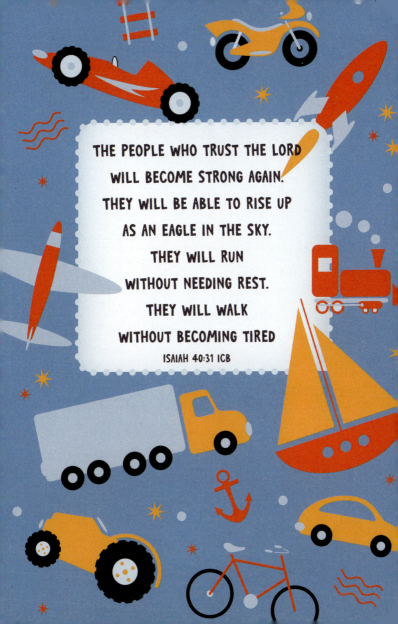

INTRODUCTION

Daily Strength for Boys is a daily devotional that helps boys like you discover how you can be brave, know God's love, and depend on him for everything you need.

In this book, you will find

- devotions that encourage you to live boldly and faithfully,
- powerful Bible verses that show God's perfect love and hope-filled promises, and
- simple prayers that help you talk with God and ask for his help.

From handling challenges to being kind and courageous, *Daily Strength for Boys* will give you tools for growing up with a strong, faith-filled heart.

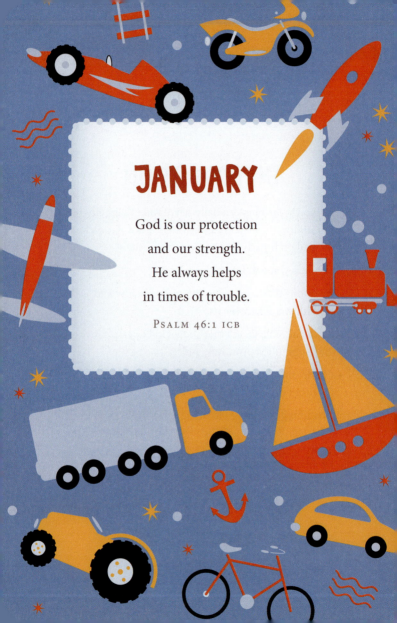

JANUARY 1

BE COURAGEOUS

> "This is my command – be strong and courageous!
> Do not be afraid or discouraged.
> For the Lord your God is with you wherever you go."
>
> JOSHUA 1:9 NLT

When we are young, life is full of new experiences. There are plenty of opportunities to be afraid. It can be scary to read in front of the class at school or get to know new friends. No matter why we are afraid, it's important to remember that God is on our side.

God is with you wherever you go. He is bigger than any scary or uncertain problem you might face. He is stronger than you can imagine, and he is always ready to help you. Talk to him about your fear, and he will give you the courage you need.

God, help me overcome my fears by remembering you are always with me. Thank you for your strength.

JANUARY 2

KNOW AND DO

I do not do the good things that I want to do. I do the bad things that I do not want to do.

ROMANS 7:19 ICB

It's a lot harder to do what is right than to know what is right. We often know exactly what we should do. The problem is that we do the wrong thing anyway. There is a constant struggle between doing what we want and doing what is right.

God does not expect you to do the right thing alone. He is always with you. The strength you need to do what is right comes from God. You can depend on him to help you when you are tempted to make the wrong decision.

God, help me do what is right. Thank you for helping me when I am tempted to do the wrong thing.

JESUS HELPS

The LORD opens the eyes of the blind.
The LORD lifts up those who are weighed down.

PSALM 146:8 NLT

When Jesus walked the earth, he was really good at noticing and helping. He saw the needs of others and he did something about it. If someone was blind, he healed them. If someone was sad, he comforted them. Jesus loved people with his words and his actions.

Jesus never changes. He still does the same things now that he did when he was on the earth. You can pray for someone who is sick or hurting and trust that Jesus will heal them. He loves to fix what is broken and find what is lost.

Jesus, thank you for caring for everybody.
I want to notice and help just like you.

JANUARY 4

GOOD GIFTS

> You have stored up so many good things.
> You have stored them up
> for those who have respect for you.
> You give those things while everyone watches.
> You give them to people who run to you for safety.
>
> PSALM 31:19 NIRV

God is storing up goodness for everyone who follows him! What exactly is that goodness? Is it safety? Is it peace? Is it a quiet heart when life is crazy? Is it joy even when your best friend is mad at you? Yes, his goodness could be all of these and much more.

God has good things in store for you. Trust in him and you will learn how much he loves you. As you follow him, he will share his heart with you. Along the way he will give you the gifts of peace, joy, and happiness.

God, help me to trust in your goodness.
Thank you for the gifts and blessings you've given me.

JANUARY 5

LEARN PATIENCE

> The Lord is good to those whose hope is in him,
> to the one who seeks him;
> it is good to wait quietly
> for the salvation of the Lord.
>
> LAMENTATIONS 3:25-26 NIV

Most people don't like waiting. Patience isn't always easy, especially when we know something good is coming. From wondering what we might get for a birthday to waiting for the last day of school, it takes practice to wait well.

God's promises won't usually follow your timeline. Sometimes you have to wait for him to answer a prayer. This isn't easy but it is good to practice waiting quietly. When you wait without being frustrated, you show that you trust God to do what he says.

God, teach me how to wait well.
Help me to trust you even when I am impatient.

JANUARY 6

STRONG ROOTS

> Let your roots grow down into him, and let your lives be built on him. Then your faith will grow strong in the truth you were taught, and you will overflow with thankfulness.
>
> COLOSSIANS 2:7 NLT

A tree with a thick trunk and solid branches has deep roots. Otherwise, the tree wouldn't be able to stand in a storm. The roots are what keep it solid and secure. Even if its branches are strong, it will topple over if it has weak roots.

Your roots also need to be sturdy. As you learn more of God's Word, the roots of your heart will grow deep and strong. Then, when you have a bad day, you won't be shaken because your faith will be steady. You will stand tall like a mighty tree, and you won't fall in the storm.

God, help my roots to grow deep and strong. Strengthen my faith as I learn more about you.

JANUARY 7

FREE TO LIVE

> Christ has set us free to enjoy our freedom. So remain strong in the faith. Don't let the chains of slavery hold you again.
>
> GALATIANS 5:1 NIRV

Without Jesus, we are stuck under the weight of our sin. Our mistakes are too heavy for us to carry, and we aren't supposed to live that way. We were made for freedom. None of us want to be imprisoned or trapped, but sometimes we forget that Jesus has set us free.

Jesus rescued you from sin. You have been given a new start because of his forgiveness. When you keep feeling guilty about your sin, it's like going back to jail and putting chains on your hands and feet. God wants you to feel free and experience the goodness of his forgiveness!

Jesus, thank you for giving me a brand-new life in you. Thank you for setting me free and taking away my guilt.

JANUARY 8

THROWN AWAY

> You will throw away all our sins
> into the deepest part of the sea.
>
> MICAH 7:19 NCV

When we do something wrong, we usually remember it for a long time. Even if we don't feel bad about what we've done, it's hard to forget. If we do feel guilty, that might feel heavy on our hearts. It's difficult to carry the weight of our mistakes.

God does not want you to carry what you aren't meant to. He wants you to give him your sins because he knows they are too heavy for you. When you surrender to him, he doesn't hold onto your sins. He throws them away! He forgets about them. When you ask him for forgiveness, he doesn't give your mistakes another thought.

God, I don't know how you can forget my sins, but I am so thankful! Thank you for your mercy and grace.

JANUARY 9

GOODNESS EVERYWHERE

> Praise the LORD, all his works
> everywhere in his dominion.
> Praise the LORD, my soul.
>
> PSALM 103:22 NIV

The world is full of God's goodness. There is evidence of his love everywhere we look. From the way the earth perfectly suits our needs to the way our bodies work, God's handiwork is wonderful!

Think about how good God is. Everything you think of is a reason to praise him. Every good gift you've ever received comes from his hands. He is the author of everything you enjoy. Praise him for all he's done.

*God, thank you for all you have done.
Help me see your goodness everywhere.*

JANUARY 10

PLANS FOR YOU

"For I know the plans I have for you," declares the LORD,
"plans to prosper you and not to harm you,
plans to give you hope and a future."

JEREMIAH 29:11 NIV

When we create something, we care what happens to it. We paint pictures and frame them for the wall. We build Lego sets and put them on shelves to admire. We build treehouses and want them to last forever. Our work matters to us.

God made you. You are his child, and he loves you so much. He created you, and he wants to be involved in your life. He cares about what happens to you. He has good plans for you. If you follow him, you will see that his plans for your future are the best.

God, thank you for taking care of me.
Help me trust your plans and follow your instructions.

JANUARY 11

GREAT RICHES

> How very rich are God's wisdom and knowledge!
> ROMANS 11:33 NIRV

God's wisdom and knowledge are the greatest riches we will ever have. They are more valuable than gold or the most precious stones. If we spend our time looking for the riches God has to offer, we will not be disappointed. They are a treasure worth searching for.

How can you search for God's wisdom and knowledge? There are many ways. You can read your Bible and ask questions about things you don't understand. You can pray everyday and spend time in God's presence. If you are looking for it, you will find God's wisdom every time.

God, thank you for the riches of your wisdom. Thank you for the knowledge you give me when I ask.

JANUARY 12

SAY THANK YOU

> The whole earth is filled with awe at your wonders;
> where morning dawns, where evening fades,
> you call forth songs of joy.
>
> PSALM 65:8 NIRV

When we see something every day, it's easy to take it for granted. We get so used to the glorious things God has made that we forget to stand in awe at what he's done. It's important to take notice of the beautiful things that surround us.

God's wonders are everywhere. If you look for them, you will find them. Take time to think about God's good works. Thank him for all the wonderful things he has done.

God, thank you for all you have made. Help me to notice what you've done even if I see it every day.

JANUARY 13

LOVE AND PRAY

"Love your enemies. Pray for those who hurt you."
MATTHEW 5:44 NIRV

We all have a natural reaction to being hurt by others. Some of us fight back, some of us run away, some of us freeze or panic, and some of us try really hard to fix it. No matter how we might respond on our own, God asks us to love and pray for the people who hurt us.

This instruction can be really hard to follow! It isn't easy to love someone who has hurt you. This is why you need God's strength. He is the only one who can love his enemies perfectly every time. His love is big enough for everyone, and he can help you love others even when they hurt you.

God, teach me to love my enemies.
I want to love like you love.

JANUARY 14

ALWAYS THANKFUL

Give thanks no matter what happens.

1 Thessalonians 5:18 NIrV

While a thunderstorm might ruin a baseball game, it's a blessing for a farmer whose crops are dry. An argument might seem stressful, but it might lead to a problem being solved. A sick day isn't often fun, but it might mean spending quality time with a parent.

Even when things don't go your way, you can practice being thankful. If you take a minute to calm down, you might notice something you didn't see before. A day that is full of difficulty can still teach you valuable lessons. There is always something to be thankful for.

God, teach me to be thankful even when I don't get my way. Help me see another side of the problem.

JANUARY 15

BIG THINGS

"Where could we get enough bread to feed this large crowd?"

MATTHEW 15:33-34 NIRV

Jesus took a little bit of bread and fish and fed thousands of people! He did a miracle right in front of all those people. Everyone who saw it knew that God was powerful and that he would take care of them.

Jesus can do big things for you too. He can take your little faith and turn it into something big. Just because you are young doesn't mean you can't trust in God for miracles. Remember that God is the same yesterday, today, and forever.

God, thank you for the encouraging stories in your Word. Help me to trust you for big things today.

JANUARY 16

GOD'S WORK

I think about the heavens.
I think about what your fingers have created.
I think about the moon and stars
that you have set in place.

PSALM 8:3 NIRV

The world is full of God's majesty. Every piece of creation tells us a story about who he is. He is strong and mighty like the mountains. He is peaceful and gentle like a stream through the woods. He is intricate and wonderful like a dewy spiderweb in the morning.

If you want to know what God is like, look at everything he's made. As your heart is filled with wonder, thank God for all he's done. He is the only one who is worthy of your praise.

God, show me your glory through creation.
Thank you for making the world so beautiful.

JANUARY 17

CONNECTED TO GOD

> "I am the vine; you are the branches. If you remain in me and I in you, you will bear much fruit; apart from me you can do nothing."
>
> JOHN 15:5 NIV

When a tree is pruned, the branches get chopped off one by one and fall to the ground. After a branch is cut from the tree, it can't live. It has been separated from the trunk and can't keep growing on its own.

You are just like that branch, and God is like the trunk of the tree. Without being connected to God, you can't grow. You need God. He is the one who helps you bear fruit. When you stay close to him, you will grow and bear fruit.

God, please give me strength today. Keep me close to you and help me grow.

JANUARY 18

HAIR COUNT

> "God even knows how many hairs are on your head. So don't be afraid."
>
> MATTHEW 10:30-31 NCV

We are so valuable to God. He even cares about the smallest details that don't really mean anything. If he cares about the small things, then he must care even more about the big things. We can find comfort in the fact that God knows us best.

It is miraculous that God knows how many hairs are on your head. He doesn't have to guess because he knows the exact number. Think about this for a moment. If God knows how many hairs are on your head, what else does he know about you? If he takes the time to know something as small as that, how must he feel about your heart?

God, thank you for taking such good care of me. Help me to remember how important I am to you.

JANUARY 19

USE YOUR VOICE

The heavens declare the glory of God;
the skies proclaim the work of his hands.
They have no speech, they use no words;
no sound is heard from them.
Yet their voice goes out into all the earth,
their words to the ends of the world.

PSALM 19:1, 3-4 NIV

The heavens and the skies can't speak, but their praise covers the whole earth. They declare God's glory. If creation can glorify God without a voice, imagine how you can praise him with all the things you say or sing!

You can talk about who he is and what he has done. You can tell your friends and family about his goodness. You can sing songs of praise to him, and you can worship him with the talents he's given you.

God, thank you for giving me a voice.
Help me to use it to worship you.

JANUARY 20

ALL TOGETHER

"In his name the nations will put their hope."
MATTHEW 12:21 NIV

You might not know a lot about history, but one thing that has always been true is that there are nations in conflict. For a lot of different reasons, there has never been a time when the whole world was at peace.

No matter what is going on in the world, you can put your hope in the name of Jesus. One day, everyone will be united with Jesus as the true king. All the nations will gather and worship him. That will be such an amazing day!

God, I am so glad I can put my hope in you! When I am discouraged by problems in the world, remind me that you are coming back to make all things new.

JANUARY 21

DEPEND ON HIM

Search me, God, and know my heart;
test me and know my anxious thoughts.
See if there is any offensive way in me,
and lead me in the way everlasting.

PSALM 139:23-24 NIV

As we get older, we are given more responsibility. We are expected to be independent and reliable. When it comes to our relationship with God, it is always best to lean on him. We don't have to rely on our own strength.

It is a good thing to need help from God all the time. He knows more about your heart than you do, and he wants to help you. When you constantly ask for help, he can lead you in the right way.

God, you are the one who knows my heart best,
and you are the one who can help me.
Teach me how to depend on you.

JANUARY 22

MADE RIGHTEOUS

The Lord is far from the wicked,
but he hears the prayers of the righteous.

PROVERBS 15:29 NLT

How can a perfect God possibly see people as good? How can we say we are righteous when we make so many mistakes? The only way to be good is to trust in Jesus' death and resurrection. When we trust in him, his perfection becomes ours.

Jesus is your righteousness. You are without fault because of what Jesus has done for you. Because of him, God is close to you and hears your prayers. Talk to him whenever you want because he will always hear you.

God, thank you for making me righteous through Jesus. Thank you for listening to me and being close to me.

JANUARY 23

POWERFUL PROTECTION

The Lord took care of them and kept them safe.
He guarded them as he would guard his own eyes.

DEUTERONOMY 32:10 NIRV

We are so important to God that he will protect us in the same way that he would protect his own eyes. When we are hurting, his heart hurts. When we are sad, he is close. He loves his children, and he wants us to be safe.

You are more than just God's creation; you are his masterpiece, his treasure, and his precious son. He is protecting you even when you don't know it. He is watching over you and keeping you safe every moment of every day.

God, thank you for protecting me and watching over me even when I don't realize it.

JANUARY 24

WHO YOU SERVE

"As for me and my family, we will serve the Lord."

JOSHUA 24:15 NLT

Sometimes our friends might make the wrong choice. When this happens, we shouldn't follow along. It's important to stand up for what's right even when we are nervous or embarrassed. We are each responsible for our own choices.

Every day you are faced with choices. Even though doing the right thing can be scary, you are the only one who can control your actions. When you are nervous, ask God for strength. He will give you the courage to serve him in all you do.

> God, I want to serve you with my whole heart. Give me strength to stand up for what is right.

JANUARY 25

A GOOD FRIEND

A friend is always loyal,
and a brother is born to help in time of need.

PROVERBS 17:17 NLT

It's wonderful to have people who are on our team. The Bible says that a friend is always loyal, and a brother helps in times of need. This is the kind of friend we should try to be.

Think about all the ways you can be a good friend. When someone is having a bad day, listen to their frustrations. When someone is overlooked, include them on purpose. When someone needs help, you can pitch in to solve a problem.

God, help me be a good friend.
Show me opportunities to be kind and helpful.

JANUARY 26

MINDFUL

Why is man important to you?
Why do you take care of human beings?

PSALM 8:4 ICB

God could have created humans and then left us alone. He could have breathed life into Adam and then watched from afar. That's not how God works. He wants to be close. He is a loving father who likes taking care of his children.

God is mindful of you. This means he thinks about you. You are always on his mind. He created you, and he cares for you. You are important to him, and he is happy to watch over you. As you turn to him, he will protect you and lead you.

God, thank you for taking care of me.
Help me remember that I am important to you.

JANUARY 27

THOUGHTFUL AND AWARE

> Don't act thoughtlessly, but understand what the Lord wants you to do.
>
> EPHESIANS 5:17 NLT

The Bible instructs us to act thoughtfully. This means we should pay attention to what is going on around us and also to what is going on inside our hearts. We don't need to hide our sin or pretend like everything is fine. Instead, we should let God help us.

When you notice something that doesn't honor God, be quick to fix it. Everyone makes mistakes, but not everyone knows how to learn from them. Ask for forgiveness and trust that God will help you when you need it.

*God, help me to be honest with you.
Teach me how to be thoughtful with my actions.*

JANUARY 28

ON DISPLAY

> What he does is glorious and splendid.
> His goodness continues forever.
>
> PSALM 111:3 ICB

God has given us a beautiful world to enjoy. If we pay attention, we will see his goodness everywhere. From a beautiful sunrise to the mightiness of the mountains, God's brilliance in on full display.

Everything God has made is good and glorious. The world is full of evidence of his love for you. Take a moment today to look around. Look at all he has done for you. In his great power he could have made the world however he wanted, but he chose to make it beautiful for you to enjoy.

God, open my eyes and help me see your glory. Thank you for the beauty of the world around me.

JANUARY 29

FULLY EQUIPPED

> Jesus has the power of God, by which he has given us everything we need to live and to serve God. We have these things because we know him. Jesus called us by his glory and goodness.
>
> 2 Peter 1:3 NCV

We all like to be prepared. It's frustrating to tackle a project without the right tools or take a test without knowing the answers. If we are faced with an impossible task, we won't be motivated to see it through.

Feeling like you can't do something the right way can be really discouraging. Knowing you don't have what you need can make you feel small, insecure, or anxious. When it comes to serving God, you have everything you need. He has already given you the right tools for the job.

God, thank you for helping me serve you. When I am discouraged, remind me that I have everything I need.

JANUARY 30

NUMBERED DAYS

> Lord, remind me how brief my time on earth will be.
> Remind me that my days are numbered—
> how fleeting my life is.
>
> Psalm 39:4 NLT

When we are young, we feel like we have all the time in the world. We see our lives spread out before us, and we feel excited about everything they might contain. It's hard to understand the idea of using our time wisely when it seems to be unlimited.

Even though it might not feel like it now, your life is short. Your time on earth is temporary, but your home in heaven is permanent; it will never end. The choices you make during your life will matter in eternity. Ask God to teach you how to spend your time wisely.

God, teach me how to use my time well.
I want to honor you with each day I have.

ALL AGES

> Don't let anyone think less of you because you are young. Be an example to all believers in what you say, in the way you live, in your love, your faith, and your purity.
>
> 1 Timothy 4:12 NLT

Grown-ups are not the only ones who have strong faith. In fact, age doesn't have anything to do with the ability to have a solid relationship with God. Anyone can love, serve, and honor him.

Your age might limit you from doing certain things like driving or having a job, but it can't limit you in your relationship with God. It doesn't matter how old you are, you can honor the Lord with everything you say and do. Your faith can inspire and encourage older people. God looks at what is in your heart, not how many years you've lived.

God, help me to be strong no matter what my age is. Teach me how to serve you even though I am young.

FEBRUARY

The name of the Lord is like a strong tower. Godly people run to it and are safe.

PROVERBS 18:10 NIRV

FEBRUARY 1

STANDING STRONG

"Man must not live only on bread. He must also live on every word that comes from the mouth of God."

MATTHEW 4:4 NIRV

When he walked the earth, Jesus went to the desert for forty days and he chose not to eat anything during that time. At one point, Satan offered him the whole world if Jesus would just turn a rock into bread. Jesus knew what the Satan was up to. He was trying to trick Jesus.

Jesus used the words of God to defeat Satan. That is exactly what you can do when you are tempted to do wrong. Read your Bible and pray. Fill your mind with God's Word, so you can use it in the battles you face. The Bible is the best weapon you have.

God, thank you for the Bible. Help me to read it and do what it says. I want to stand strong against the enemy.

FEBRUARY 2

BE CONFIDENT

Because of Christ and our faith in him, we can now come boldly and confidently into God's presence.

EPHESIANS 3:12 NLT

A small child doesn't understand or recognize titles. The child of a celebrity or a famous politician doesn't care about their parent's job or position. All the child knows is that their parent loves them and takes care of them.

Jesus said that you can come to him like a little child. This means that you don't need to be afraid of him or worry about what he will think of you. You don't need to be intimidated by his title. You can just be yourself. Be confident and talk to Jesus about anything!

God, I am so glad that you hear me and answer me. Help me remember I can come to you about anything.

FEBRUARY 3

HE REJOICES

"Rejoice with me;
I have found my lost sheep."

LUKE 15:6 NIV

It feels so good to find something that was lost! We feel happy when we find something even if it is small, like a favorite pencil, book, or pair of sunglasses. If we feel so much delight over finding a missing toy, imagine how God feels when one of his children finds their way to him.

God cares deeply about you. When you decide to follow him, he is so excited! He celebrates every time you take a step toward him. You matter so much to him, and he is overjoyed when you choose to be with him.

God, I am thankful for your love. Thank you for being like a good shepherd who always looks for his lost sheep.

FEBRUARY 4

EVERY DAY

> The LORD has given, and the LORD has taken away.
> May the name of the LORD be praised.
>
> JOB 1:21 NIRV

No one gets what they want all the time. We all have times where we can see so many of God's blessings, and we all have times when we struggle to see anything good at all. God is always in control. Even when we think nothing is going the right way, God is still worthy of our praise.

Give God your praise on good days and on bad days. Even though your life might be different every day, God never changes. He is always the same, and he deserves your gratitude.

God, you are in control of my life. Thank you for taking care of me on good and bad days.

FEBRUARY 5

FOLLOW THE SPIRIT

> We have received the Spirit who is from God. The Spirit helps us understand what God has freely given us.
>
> 1 CORINTHIANS 2:12 NIRV

After Jesus was raised from the dead, he went back to heaven to be with God. Before he left, he gave us a wonderful gift. He left his Holy Spirit so that we wouldn't be alone. He knew that life would be difficult and that we would need someone to guide and encourage us.

When you chose to follow Jesus, he gave you his Spirit. You are never ever alone. No matter what, you have the Spirit to help you. Instead of wondering what to do, you can ask him for help. He will encourage you and teach you about Jesus.

God, thank you for the gift of the Holy Spirit. Help me to follow him as he points me toward you.

FEBRUARY 6

SING PRAISE

Sing praises to God. Sing praises.
Sing praises to our King. Sing praises.
God is King of all the earth.
So sing a song of praise to him.

PSALM 47:6-7 ICB

God created each of us with a voice that can praise him. It is good to worship him and acknowledge all the good things he has done. When we praise him, we strengthen our faith, and our hearts are transformed in his presence.

No matter what your voice sounds like, it is delightful to God. He loves it when you offer him your praise. If you're not sure what to say, think about some things you are thankful for. Make a list and talk to him about it.

God, you are the king of all the earth. You have been good to me. Help me to sing and speak of your goodness!

FEBRUARY 7

FULFILL YOUR PURPOSE

We know that in all things God works for the good of those who love him, who have been called according to his purpose.

ROMANS 8:28 NIV

When we are young, we spend a lot of time thinking about the future. We imagine the type of job we might have or the way our family might look. We think about our future house and car. We imagine the places we'll visit and the trips we will take.

God has a purpose for your life. No matter what your future looks like, your greatest purpose is to seek him. He wants you to do things you love, and he wants you to do those things while you love and follow him. Choose to love God with all your heart, and you will stay on the right path.

God, when I feel lost, let me find purpose in loving and serving you.

FEBRUARY 8

ASK FOR HELP

> I asked the LORD for help, and he answered me.
> He saved me from all that I feared.
> Those who go to him for help are happy,
> and they are never disgraced.
>
> PSALM 34:4-5 NCV

Good parents know what their children need. Not only do they know what they need but they happily provide it. God is the very best father there is. He knows exactly what we need, from the clothes we wear to the friendships we want, and he joyfully provides it.

It is good to ask God for help. Don't be ashamed or embarrassed. Run to him and tell him exactly what you need. As you depend on him, you will experience the peace of his presence. Ask him for help because he loves to take care of you.

God, thank you for knowing what I need. Remind me that I can always ask you for help.

FEBRUARY 9

LIGHT OF JESUS

"Let the light shine out of the darkness!"

2 CORINTHIANS 4:6 ICB

Nothing good comes from hiding in the darkness. When we keep our sins hidden, we don't get to experience the freedom that Jesus gives us. His death means we don't have to carry the heavy weight of our sins anymore.

When Jesus comes into your heart, he fills it with light. Nothing is hidden. His light takes away the darkness. You don't ever have to be embarrassed about your mistakes. He sees you clearly, and he is not ashamed of you.

God, thank you for forgiving my sins.
Help me not to try to hide my mistakes from you.

FEBRUARY 10

GOD SEES

> "I know what you do. I know about your love, your faith, your service, and your patience."
>
> REVELATION 2:19 ICB

We won't always get recognized for the good things we do. People don't always say thank you, and they may not notice our hard work. It's important to make good decisions even when no one will see. We honor God when we choose to do the right thing no matter what.

God sees everything you do. He notices your hard work, and he will reward you for it. It doesn't matter if people recognize your actions when you know that God is on your side.

God, thank you for seeing me. Help me to remember that your opinion matters more than anyone else's.

FEBRUARY 11

GUILTY FEELINGS

> Evil people run even though no one is chasing them.
> But good people are as brave as a lion.
>
> PROVERBS 28:1 ICB

It's normal to feel guilty when we've done something wrong. Instead of avoiding guilt, we can look at it like a reminder to change the path we're on. If we don't pay attention to guilt, we might continue to do the wrong thing.

When you feel guilty for doing something wrong, remember that God is on your side. Be brave and tell the truth. God can handle your mistakes. When you confess your sins and ask for forgiveness, God will take away your guilt.

Dear God, help me run to you when I mess up. I don't want to carry guilt when I can give it to you instead.

FEBRUARY 12

SPEAK UP

> Who will help me fight against the wicked?
> Who will stand with me against those who do evil?
>
> PSALM 94:16 ICB

As followers of Jesus, we are supposed to value justice and kindness. Jesus always stood up for people who were ignored or bullied. He made people feel important when the whole world said they were useless.

It is good to stand up for what is right. When you see someone being mean, speak up and defend the person who is being hurt. Be kind and stand up for the truth just like Jesus did. If you ask him, he will give you the courage to do what is right.

God, help me stand up for what is right. Help me to be brave and give me the right words to say.

FEBRUARY 13

ASK FOR HELP

> Plans fail without good advice.
> But plans succeed when you get advice
> from many others.
>
> PROVERBS 15:22 ICB

Most things in life are better with a little help. Even when we think we can do something alone, it's good to listen to the advice of others. We all think a little bit differently, and it helps to have more than one point of view.

It is good to ask for help. It makes other people feel important, and it helps you to succeed. It doesn't make sense to do something alone when someone else already knows how to do it. Don't be shy when it comes to admitting you don't know something.

God, teach me to ask for help instead of doing things alone. Help me to love good advice.

FEBRUARY 14

ALREADY RICH

I have learned to be satisfied with the things I have and with everything that happens.

PHILIPPIANS 4:11 ICB

When we get what we want, it usually isn't long before we turn our attention to something different. This is called being dissatisfied. Instead of thinking about what we don't have, we should focus on being thankful for what we do have.

Getting something new might seem like it will make you happy, but pretty soon you'll want something else. It is better to learn to be happy with the blessings you have. Think about reasons to be thankful, and you will find that you are already rich.

> God, teach me to be happy with what I have.
> You have given me so many good things.

FEBRUARY 15

GOD'S WAY

> "I will make you wise. I will show you where to go.
> I will guide you and watch over you."
>
> PSALM 32:8-9 ICB

We all have people in our lives we look up to. We trust their decisions, and we ask them for help when we need it. If we can follow the example set by a person, how much more can we trust God?

You can follow him and trust everything he does because he knows what is best for you. Every choice he makes is good and right. You don't ever have to doubt him because everything he says is perfect.

*God, help me to follow you closely.
Your ways are always best.*

FEBRUARY 16

ATTITUDE CHECK

Do everything without complaining or arguing.

PHILIPPIANS 2:14 ICB

It's not always easy to do the right thing. It's normal to whine or complain when we don't get our way, but this isn't how the Bible tells us to live. Instead, we are supposed to do everything without complaining or arguing.

It's not right to have a bad attitude just because you don't want to do something. It's important to learn how to share what you think without complaining or arguing. It takes practice, but you can joyfully do your best even when you don't want to.

Dear God, help me to do things without complaining. Fill me with joy and help me to have a good attitude.

FEBRUARY 17

GREAT MERCY

> God loves us deeply. He is full of mercy. So he gave us new life because of what Christ has done. He gave us life even when we were dead in sin. God's grace has saved you.
>
> EPHESIANS 2:4-5 NIRV

Mercy is giving someone something they do not deserve or didn't earn. God is full of mercy for his children. Through Jesus, he made a way for us to be free. We can never earn salvation. We can only accept it as a gift of mercy.

Even on days when you only make mistakes or wrong choices, God's mercy toward you is still great. As you learn about God's mercy, you can begin to show it to others. This means being kind when someone else isn't or forgiving others when they have hurt you.

Thank you for your mercy, God. As I learn more about your mercy, help me to show it to others.

SHARING YOUR FAITH

"Whoever acknowledges me before others, I will also acknowledge before my Father in heaven."

MATTHEW 10:32 NIV

Faith is meant to be shared. Loving Jesus is not something we are supposed to keep to ourselves. God asks us to share the good news of the gospel because he wants everyone to hear it.

When you have the chance to share the truth, ask the Holy Spirit to help you. He will guide you and give you the right words to say. If you are shy, ask God for courage. He will teach you how to speak boldly.

God, I don't want to keep my faith to myself. Help me to know when to share about you and give me the words to say.

FEBRUARY 19

TAKE A BREAK

A little sleep, a little slumber,
a little folding of the hands to rest.

PROVERBS 24:33 NIV

We all need rest. God could have created us to stay awake all night and to never need a break, but he didn't. He gave us the need for sleep. He gave us bodies that have to slow down and recharge.

Rest is a good gift from God! Sometimes when you are upset or frustrated, all you need is some rest. In those times, take a deep breath and find a quiet place to take a break. Practicing rest is one way you can honor God for the way he made you.

God, help me to honor you by resting. Teach me how to take a break when I am overwhelmed.

FEBRUARY 20

BEYOND EVERYTHING

> I pray that you and all God's holy people will have the power to understand the greatness of Christ's love—how wide and how long and how high and how deep that love is.
>
> EPHESIANS 3:18 NCV

God's love is deeper than the oceans. It is higher than the tallest mountain and wider than the open skies. God's love for his people is greater than we can ever imagine. It goes beyond anything we can understand on our own.

Through God's great mercy, you get to experience his love. Even when you don't deserve it, his love still covers you. Even when you are at your worst, his love stays. There is nothing you can do to change how big God's love is. No matter what, it will always be wider, longer, higher, and deeper than you can imagine.

Thank you for your love, God. Thank you for loving me even when I don't deserve it.

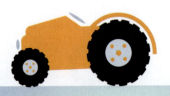

FEBRUARY 21

THE FORGOTTEN

> When widows are in trouble, take care of them. Do the same for children who have no parents.
>
> JAMES 1:27 NIRV

There are many people who cannot take care of themselves. They are alone and don't have anyone to help them. These are the people that God takes special care of. He doesn't forget them, and he doesn't abandon them. He wants us to notice them and love them like he does.

The Bible says that caring for people who are forgotten is more important than following a list of rules. You can do everything right all day long, but if you don't love others, it doesn't matter. Do your best to notice people others have forgotten.

God, help me to do what pleases you. I want to see people who need your love.

FEBRUARY 22

HE UNDERSTANDS

He was tempted in every way that we are, but he did not sin.

HEBREWS 4:15 NCV

Jesus understands every problem we face. He is not surprised by our frustrations or confused by our struggles. He doesn't make us feel bad about our mistakes, and he doesn't point his finger at us and demand we do better.

Jesus knows what it is like to walk the earth. He knows how it feels to be hurt, frustrated, angry, or confused. When you are struggling, he doesn't want you to be stuck in guilt. He wants you to run to him and ask him for strength. He wants to put you on the right path and lead you every step of the way.

Jesus, I'm so glad you know how I feel. When I sin, help me turn to you quickly.

FEBRUARY 23

GOD CAN DO IT

> Summon your power, God;
> show us your strength, our God,
> as you have done before.
>
> PSALM 68:28 NIV

The Bible is not just a book of stories. It is a record of things God has done. It is full of examples of him using his power and displaying his glory.

When you know what God can do, your prayers can line up with that. If he did a miracle once, he could do it again. You know that he can feed the hungry, heal the sick, and raise the dead because his Word says he can. You can ask God to do mighty things because you know he already has.

God, I know you are big and strong! I know you can do mighty things because you have done them before.

FEBRUARY 24

RESPECTED

God is able to do far more than we could ever ask for or imagine.

EPHESIANS 3:20 NIRV

God does not have limits. Nothing can beat him. He is better than anything we could ever imagine. He can do things we can't even dream of. His power and love are bigger than we could ever understand.

There is nothing in your life that is too hard for God. There is no problem that he cannot solve. There isn't a mess he cannot untangle. No matter what is going on, God can make things clear and new. He is big enough to help every time.

God, you are strong and able! Help me solve the problems that are too big for me.

FEBRUARY 25

BEING HAPPY

> I have learned the secret of being happy at any time in everything that happens. I have learned to be happy when I have all that I need and when I do not have the things I need.
>
> PHILIPPIANS 4:12 ICB

In the Bible, Paul says that the secret to being happy is to be content with what we have. This means that we don't look at our lives and focus on what's missing. Instead, we think about what we are thankful for.

When you start comparing yourself to others, you can feel like your life isn't good enough. There will always be someone who is doing something more exciting or has something you want. Finding contentment means being happy with what you have already been given.

God, I want to be content. Teach me how to be happy with what I have.

FEBRUARY 26

MEEK NOT WEAK

People shouted at him and made fun of him. But he didn't do the same thing back to them. When he suffered, he didn't say he would make them suffer. Instead, he trusted in the God who judges fairly.

1 PETER 2:23 NIRV

When we are meek, it means we do not insist on our way. Even when it would make sense to fight, we choose peace and kindness. Jesus is the perfect example of meekness. He had the power to fight off his enemies, but he chose not to.

Jesus loved others completely even when they were horrible to him. This is the example you are supposed to follow. It's not easy, but with God's help, you can love others in that way.

God, it's hard to be meek, but I know it honors you. Help me to love others even when it is hard.

FEBRUARY 27

ENDURE

> The Lord is good. His faithful love continues forever.
> It will last for all time to come.
>
> PSALM 100:5 NIRV

The love of God has no end. He will never grow tired of us, and he will never stop loving us. We don't really understand the concept of forever. Everything we know is limited. We change our minds often, and we don't understand eternity the way God does.

Nothing on earth lasts forever, but God's love for you does. It can never be taken from you. It will last for all eternity. Praise him for loving you so much you can't even comprehend it.

> God, thank you for your unending faithfulness. Help me to understand how much you love me.

FEBRUARY 28

TRUSTWORTHY

> You will keep in perfect peace
> all who trust in you,
> all whose thoughts are fixed on you!
>
> ISAIAH 26:3 NLT

God is trustworthy. This means he is true to his word. All throughout the Bible we can see examples of how he kept his promises. If he did it once, he will do it again because he never changes.

When you trust God, you will have peace. When you know he is in control, you don't have to worry. He wants to help you with each problem you face. Talk to him about your troubles and let him calm your fears.

*God, I want your peace in my heart.
Help me to trust in you more each day.*

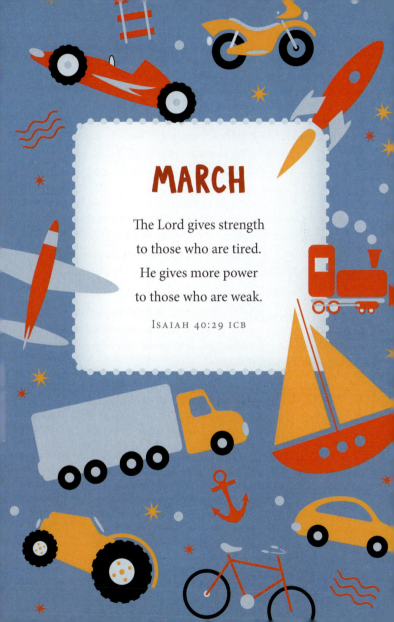

MARCH

The Lord gives strength to those who are tired. He gives more power to those who are weak.

ISAIAH 40:29 ICB

MARCH 1

GET READY

Remember, the Lord is coming soon. Don't worry about anything; instead, pray about everything. Tell God what you need, and thank him for all he has done.

PHILIPPIANS 4:5-6 NLT

When we have someone coming to visit, we often take time to get ready. We might clean up our room or plan something to eat. When we know a guest is on the way, we can make sure we are prepared. It's exciting to get ready for their arrival.

Jesus has promised that he is coming back. One day, he will return and make all things new. While you are waiting, remember there are things to do. Be kind to people, show the love of God to others, and pray about everything. Get ready for the return of Jesus!

God, I am excited about Jesus coming back! Help me to prepare for his return.

MARCH 2

GIVE STRENGTH

Encourage each other and give each other strength, just as you are doing now.

1 Thessalonians 5:11 NCV

Relationships are a wonderful gift. We can support each other when life is hard, and we can share our joy when our blessings overflow. It's beautiful to walk through life with people who love you no matter what.

Think about the people God has put in your life. You can encourage the people around you and help them when they are weak. You can tell them what you love about them, listen when they are sad, or do something nice for them on purpose.

God, thank you for the people who have helped me. Help me to be a blessing to the people around me.

MARCH 3

ACCEPT OTHERS

Christ accepted you, so you should accept each other, which will bring glory to God.

ROMANS 15:7 NCV

When we accept others, we don't look at everything they do wrong. We don't focus only on our differences. We don't decide who is worthy of love and who isn't.

God asks you to accept other people. This means that you love everyone you meet no matter how different they are. Just because someone doesn't like the same things as you, doesn't mean they are not interesting. Just because someone has different opinions than you do, doesn't mean they are not smart.

God, you never leave me out or ignore what I have to say. Teach me how to accept others as you have accepted me.

MARCH 4

CREATOR OF ALL

> "You are worthy because you created all things.
> They were created and they exist.
> This is the way you planned it."
>
> REVELATION 4:11 NIRV

Everything we can see has been created by God. The sun and the moon were his idea. The earth and everything in it fit together perfectly because he has made it so. Every animal, plant, element, and person are here because of his intelligence, power, and kindness.

Of everything he created, we are the most important. We were made in his image, and we are precious to him. He is happy with the way he created you. Praise him for all the wonderful things he has made.

God, I praise you for everything you have created! Thank you for all the wonderful things you have made.

MARCH 5

ALWAYS MERCIFUL

The Lord wants to show his mercy to you.
He wants to rise and comfort you.
The Lord is a fair God.
And everyone who waits for his help will be happy.

Isaiah 30:18 icb

Mercy is another word for great kindness or compassion. When we choose gentleness instead of being harsh, that is mercy. When we decide to forgive someone even when they do the wrong thing, that is mercy.

God has so much mercy for you. He is strong and powerful, and everything he does is right. Instead of being annoyed by your mistakes, he shows you mercy. He lifts you up and hugs you even when you do the wrong thing. He is kind and loving.

God, thank you for showing me mercy. Help me to be kind to others because of your love.

MARCH 6

GIVE LIFE

As a tree gives fruit,
healing words give life.

PROVERBS 15:4 NCV

The words we say are a big deal. We can give life and bring healing by saying the right thing to someone who is hurting. Healing words don't shame people. They don't hurt. Healing words are full of light, goodness, and strength.

When you know someone who is hurting, your words are your strongest weapon. You can pray for them. You can encourage them to keep going, tell them God is good, and comfort them.

*God, teach me how to speak healing words.
I want to give life to others.*

MARCH 7

WATCHING OVER YOU

> He will not let you be defeated.
> He who guards you never sleeps.
>
> PSALM 121:3 ICB

We all need sleep. Our bodies need rest, and our minds need a break. When we close our eyes and our bodies rest, God is keeping his watchful eyes on us. Just because we are unaware, doesn't mean God checks out.

The Bible says that God never sleeps. He is able to watch over you every single moment of the day and night! He never takes a break from guarding you. You can rest knowing that he is on your side.

God, thank you for watching over me.
Thank you for keeping me safe while I sleep.

MARCH 8

MONEY MONSTER

Keep your lives free from the love of money. And be satisfied with what you have.

HEBREWS 13:5 ICB

Money is a great thing to have, but the Bible warns us not to love it too much. It's easy to become greedy and selfish if we aren't careful. When we always want something new, it is time to focus on being thankful for what we have.

Have you ever thought about how you can serve others with your money? You could buy a gift for someone or help a friend. If you practice being generous now, it will be easier to do when you are older and have more money.

God, I want to be generous like you.
Thank you for giving me what I need.

MARCH 9

WORK HARD

> The lazy will not get what they want,
> but those who work hard will.
>
> PROVERBS 13:4 NCV

We were created to have a purpose. Even though sometimes it is nice to do nothing, we are most satisfied when we work toward something. We were made to have goals and then take steps toward them.

It is good to work hard. It is good for your mind and your body. When a job needs to be done, be the kind of person who does it well without complaining.

Dear God, help me to work hard
and not complain.

MARCH 10

WORK IN PROGRESS

> God began doing a good work in you, and I am sure he will continue it until it is finished when Jesus Christ comes again.
>
> PHILIPPIANS 1:6 NCV

God created each of us, and he loves to guide us through life. When we do something wrong, he does not give up on us. He sees us with love, and he is always ready to help us grow.

God is always working on you. For the rest of your life, you will continue to learn and change. Don't worry about the things you don't know, or the skills you don't have. Trust that God will keep you on the right path.

God, thank you for loving me every day no matter what.

MARCH 11

COME TOGETHER

"If two or three people come together in my name, I am there with them."

Matthew 18:20 ncv

Parents love when their children get along. When kids are kind to each other, it brings joy. God is like this with his children too. He loves it when we work together.

When you gather together with other people who love Jesus, God is with you. When you pray together or serve others in God's name, he promises to be close to you.

> God, thank you for being close to me. I want to honor you by working well with others.

MARCH 12

BE HOPEFUL

> Be strong and don't lose hope.
> Wait for the Lord.
>
> PSALM 27:14 NCV

When we have hope it means we are waiting for something good to happen. We put our hope in God because he has promised to make everything new when Jesus comes back.

No matter what happens, God will keep his promises. Even if you have the worst day you can imagine, you can still have hope because one day Jesus will solve every problem forever. Hope is what helps you stay strong when things don't go the way you want them to.

God, fill me with hope. Teach me how to wait patiently for your promises.

MARCH 13

FACE TO FACE

> Now we see a dim reflection, as if we were looking into a mirror, but then we shall see clearly.
>
> 1 CORINTHIANS 13:12 NCV

It's hard to see through windows that are foggy, and we cannot see our reflection in a mirror that is smudged or steamed up. Knowing God is a little bit like that. We know he is close, but we cannot see him clearly.

One day you will see God face-to-face in heaven, but until then you can know him by looking at Jesus. The Bible says that everything Jesus said and did was a perfect reflection of God. If you want to know God, learn about Jesus.

God, I want to know you even though I can't see you fully. Teach me about who you are.

MARCH 14

HARD WORK

Those who work hard make a profit,
but those who only talk will be poor.

PROVERBS 14:23 NCV

Planning is important, and it's good to have a clear idea of how you will finish a job. It's important to spend time organizing our work, but at some point, we have to do more than talk.

When something needs to be done, you can't just talk about it. You have to do the work. Complaining will only make the job take longer. Instead of wasting time, just get the job done.

God, I want to be a hard worker. When I am tempted to complain, help me focus on what I need to do.

MARCH 15

SAFE WITH HIM

> You are my hiding place.
> You protect me from my troubles.
>
> PSALM 32:7 NCV

There is no guarantee that life will be easy. Even if we do all the right things, there will still be problems we cannot control. We can't control how other people behave, and we can't control what happens in the world.

Even if everything goes wrong, God can be a hiding place for you. He protects you and keeps you safe. He is always there for you. When you face problems, God wants to comfort you and help you through them.

God, thank you for being my hiding place. When problems come up, remind me I am safe with you.

MARCH 16

SING TO GOD

> Sing a new song to him;
> play well and joyfully.
>
> PSALM 33:1, 3 NCV

When we worship God with songs, we take the focus off ourselves. Instead of thinking about our problems or complaints, we look at God. When we use our voices to praise him, our attitude will follow.

God loves it when you sing songs to him. He loves to hear your voice. The more you praise God, the more your heart will feel close to him. When you are close to him, he fills you with his love.

God, thank you for loving my voice.
Give me a joyful song to sing.

MARCH 17

EVERY NEED

My God will meet all your needs according to the riches of his glory in Christ Jesus.

PHILIPPIANS 4:19 NIV

God can meet all our needs because he has unlimited resources. This means there is no end to what he has or what he can do. He created the entire universe just with his words. Imagine what else he can do.

Meeting your needs is not hard for God. He loves it when you ask him for help. He loves to give his children good gifts. Everything God has is yours because you are his son. Ask him for what you need, knowing that he can do it.

God, thank you for taking care of me.
Help me to be thankful for all you have done.

MARCH 18

TRUST AND FOLLOW

> It was by faith Abraham obeyed God's call to go to another place God promised to give him.
>
> HEBREWS 11:8 NCV

There are many times that we don't know what to do. It's not always easy to make decisions, and we don't know exactly what is ahead. This is why it's important to trust God with each step we take.

Abraham in the Bible is a great example of what it means to trust God. He didn't know where he was going, but he knew he could follow God. Even when you don't understand the path you are on, trust that God will keep his promises to you.

God, help me to trust and follow you. When I am confused, help me remember your promises.

MARCH 19

MOST IMPORTANT

"Martha, Martha, you are worried and upset about many things. Only one thing is important. Mary has chosen the better thing, and it will never be taken away from her."

LUKE 10:41-42 NCV

Mary and her sister Martha were friends with Jesus. One day, Martha was focused on finishing her to-do list and making sure that everything was just right. Mary was focused on learning from Jesus. Mary knew that spending time with Jesus was more important than anything else she had to do.

Being with Jesus is the most important part of your day too. From the moment you wake up in the morning, you can spend time with him. You can talk to him about your day as you brush your teeth, and you can ask him for help as you go through the day.

God, spending time with you is what is best for me. Help me to put you first in all that I do.

MARCH 20

A FATHER'S GIFTS

> "Even though you are evil, you know how to give good gifts to your children. How much more will your Father who is in heaven give good gifts to those who ask him!"
>
> MATTHEW 7:11 NIRV

We all have people in our lives who love us very much. They make us feel safe and cared for. If people who make mistakes can love us well, imagine how perfect God's love is! He loves to take care of us, and he loves to give us good gifts.

God is happy when you ask him for what you need because he loves to care for you. A good father gets joy from giving gifts to his children, and God is your perfect Father. Today, talk to him about what you need and what you want. God loves to hear from you.

Thank you, God, for giving me good gifts. Help me to ask you for what I need and want.

MARCH 21

GOOD WORKS

> How many are your works, LORD!
> In wisdom you made them all.
>
> PSALM 104:24 NIV

It is impossible for us to know all the amazing things God is doing. Our minds can't understand all of his works, but if you ask him, he will show you. He will open your eyes to see what he is doing.

As you notice God moving, you can praise him. You might start seeing how he takes care of you or how he has provided for you. You might begin to discover how beautiful the world is. You might begin to notice how much he loves you. Ask him to show you what he is doing, and he will!

God, thank you for all that you do! Help me to notice how you are working each day.

MARCH 22

ONE IN A BILLION

> "There is joy in the presence of God's angels when even one sinner repents."
>
> LUKE 15:10 NLT

There are more than seven billion people alive right now, and God cares for each and every one. Each person is equally important to God. Even if all but one turned to follow him, he would still wait for the last one.

God cares deeply for every single one of his children. You are one of those children. You are loved and cared for by the Creator of the universe, and he is delighted that you are following him.

God, thank you for seeing me. Surround me with your love and fill my heart with confidence and peace.

MARCH 23

SHARING IN LOVE

Because we loved you, we were happy to share God's Good News with you. But not only that, we were also happy to share even our own lives with you.

1 Thessalonians 2:8 icb

We can love others by sharing God's truth with them. It is good to look for opportunities to share our faith with those around us. When we love someone, we want good things for them. There is no better gift than understanding God's love.

As you learn more about God, you can share with others. Tell your friends and family about what God is doing in your life. Share what you love about him and how he makes you feel. Talk about who he is and the good things he has done.

Thank you, God, for the chance to show love to others by talking about you.

MARCH 24

BE BRAVE

"Be strong and brave."
DEUTERONOMY 31:6 NIRV

God asked many people in Scripture to do impossible things. Every time he told them to be brave, he reassured them he would be with them the whole time. Anytime he asked his people to be strong, he also reminded them he would be their strength.

God is on your side. He is with you all of the time, and he knows exactly what you need. He doesn't command you to be brave and then leave you alone to figure it out. He says to be brave and courageous because he is always there to help.

God, you are my strength! I can be brave because you are always with me.

MARCH 25

GENEROUS

Anyone who is kind to poor people lends to the Lord.
God will reward them for what they have done.

PROVERBS 19:17 NIRV

The world is full of people who don't have what they need. Some people don't have enough food to eat, and some people don't have anywhere to live. God says that these people are very important. He says that everyone is valuable no matter how much money they have.

If something is important to God, it should be important to you. There is always room to share. When you are generous with what you have, whether it's a little or a lot, you show other people how God feels about them.

God, help me to be generous like you.
Help me notice the needs of those around me.

MARCH 26

UNBROKEN

A cheerful heart makes you healthy.
But a broken spirit dries you up.

PROVERBS 17:22 NIRV

God doesn't ask us to be happy and smiley all the time. He knows that sometimes we will suffer or experience pain. He wants us to turn to him on all sorts of days. Even on our hardest days, we can trust God to keep our spirits from breaking.

God is with you on your worst days, and he will comfort you when life is hard. He is the one who can lift your spirit and give you joy.

God, thank you for turning sadness into joy.

MARCH 27

BETTER PATH

> Think carefully about the paths that your feet walk on. Always choose the right ways.
>
> PROVERBS 4:26 NIRV

It's always easier to follow a well-worn path than to stumble through the woods. When we follow the path, we are less likely to get lost. It is safer and wiser to stay on a road that is clearly marked.

In the same way, God has created a path of truth for you to walk. He knows exactly what your life looks like, and he will faithfully guide you if you let him. As long as you are following him, you will always be on the right path.

God, help me to follow you closely. I want to stay on the path of truth.

MARCH 28

UNAFRAID

> Anyone who shows respect for the Lord
> has a strong tower.
> It will be a safe place for their children.
>
> Proverbs 14:26 nirv

We can respect God by believing what he says and doing our best to follow him each day. When we respect God, he promises to keep us safe. His presence is the safest place we can be.

God pays attention to your fears. He doesn't tell you they're silly, and he doesn't tell you to get over it. His Word says he will protect you and comfort you. As you follow him, you will learn he is always by your side.

*God, I trust you with my fears.
Keep me safe and secure.*

MARCH 29

SPRINGTIME MIRACLE

Then the angel spoke to the women. "Don't be afraid!" he said. "I know you are looking for Jesus, who was crucified. He isn't here! He is risen from the dead, just as he said would happen."

MATTHEW 28:5-6 NCV

Easter is a time to celebrate newness. All around us, the world is bursting into life after a long winter. Springtime feels like the perfect time to celebrate Jesus' resurrection. As the grass turns green again and the flowers start to bloom, we remember that Jesus died and rose again.

Jesus did a great and marvelous thing. He took your sins and paid the price for them so you could be close to God. Your sins are no longer in the way. Because of Jesus, you can have new life every single day.

Jesus, thank you for the way spring reminds me of the new life I have in you.

MARCH 30

BLOTTED OUT

> Have mercy on me, O God,
> because of your unfailing love.
> Because of your great compassion,
> blot out the stain of my sins.
>
> PSALM 51:1 NLT

Even on our best days, we still aren't perfect. We all make mistakes, and we choose to do the wrong thing. We don't deserve the forgiveness of God, but he washes away our sin anyway.

When you blot out a stain, it's like it was never there. The piece of clothing looks fresh and clean without a spot to be seen. This is how God treats your sin. When you ask him for forgiveness, he wipes away your sin until it can't be seen at all.

God, thank you for taking care of my sin and making me clean.

MARCH 31

GOD'S STORY

> He provided the way for people to be made pure from sin. Then he sat down at the right hand of the King, the Majesty in heaven.
>
> HEBREWS 1:3 NIRV

A good story draws us in and makes us feel like we are part of that world. We learn about the characters, and we excitedly follow along as new details are revealed. We look forward to a victorious ending or the conclusion of a great adventure.

God has created an incredible story that you get to be a part of. You are in the middle of an intricate reality, woven together by the Creator of the universe. From when Adam breathed his first breath until the return of Jesus, God has been at work.

God, thank you for the story you've created. Help me to see how you are always at work.

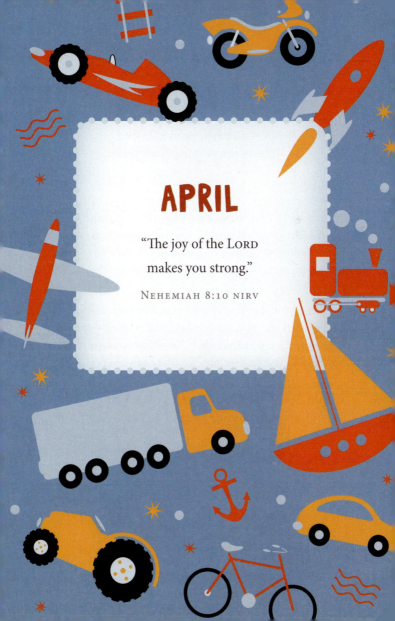

APRIL

"The joy of the Lord makes you strong."

Nehemiah 8:10 nirv

APRIL 1

FEAR THE LORD

> Happy is the person who fears the Lord.
> He loves what the Lord commands.
>
> PSALM 112:1 ICB

When we fear the Lord, we love him and respect his instructions. This is because we know who he is, and we believe what he says is true. When you respect him, and choose to accept his love, you will want to obey him from your heart.

Following God makes you truly happy because he knows what is best for you. This doesn't mean that you will feel happy all the time, but it means that you will have contentment deep in your heart. There is nothing on earth that can give you that feeling like God can.

God, teach me how to fear you. Give me grace to follow your commands and do what you say.

APRIL 2

UNFAIR WINNERS

> Don't be upset when other people succeed.
> Don't be upset when they carry out their evil plans.
>
> Psalm 37:7 NIrV

Sometimes bad things happen. The good guy doesn't always succeed, and the hero doesn't always win the battle. There are times in life when everything seems unfair. It's hard to watch people win when they are hurting others in the process.

When this happens, God says to trust him. He promises to take care of injustice. In the end, he will be victorious. His plans will prosper, and he will win forever. You are his son, and no matter what happens during your life, you will win in the end too.

God, I trust your plans! Help me to depend on you when everything seems unfair.

APRIL 3

FAITH NOT WORKS

> When people work, their wages are not a gift, but something they have earned. But people are counted as righteous, not because of their work, but because of their faith in God who forgives sinners.
>
> ROMANS 4:4-5 NLT

When we work hard in this world, we get paid for it. We give up our time, energy, and skills, and we get money in return. Without a job, we can't pay for the things we need in life.

Jesus' love is like money that you didn't have to work for! He gives you forgiveness and eternal life, and you don't have to do anything but believe in him to get it. He gives you everything you need because of your faith in God.

God, thank you for the gift of Jesus' love. Help me to remember I don't need to work for what you give me.

APRIL 4

GREAT HELPER

The Lord is good.
He gives protection in times of trouble.
He knows who trusts in him.

NAHUM 1:7 ICB

God is with us when life is easy, and he is with us when our days are dark. In times of trouble, God is a safe place for those who trust in him. He is always near when we are struggling.

God is your strength and your great helper. When you make mistakes, he wants to help you make things right. He is by your side, and he will help you every step of the way. No matter what happens, God is always good.

God, I trust in your goodness. Help me to run to you for help when I am in trouble.

APRIL 5

THE GOOD FATHER

"I will be your father, and you will be my sons and daughters, says the Lord All-Powerful."

2 CORINTHIANS 6:18 ICB

God is a good father. He is strong, protective, and he loves his children more than we can understand. He is all powerful, and we can trust him to take care of everything he has created. The earth and everything in it belong to him.

You are a son of God. He created you, and he loves you. He is proud of who you are. When he looks at you, he is not angry, frustrated, or disappointed. He knows you better than anyone else, and his love for you is unending.

Thank you, God, that you are a good father, and that you love me as your child.

APRIL 6

RESIST AND WIN

Submit yourselves, then, to God. Resist the devil, and he will flee from you.

JAMES 4:7 NIV

Every day is filled with choices. We get to decide if we are going to follow God with our actions or not. It's important to realize that we are responsible for the decisions we make. If we want to honor God, we need to do the right thing on purpose.

You might have realized that doing the right thing isn't always easy. Sometimes you have to fight to make good choices. This means doing the right thing even when you really don't want to. The Bible promises that when you choose good, evil will run far from you.

God, give me strength to do the right thing. Help me resist the devil and honor you instead.

APRIL 7

GOOD EXAMPLES

A huge cloud of witnesses is all around us.

HEBREWS 12:1 NIRV

The great cloud of witnesses is the collection of people who were faithful to God for all their days. History is filled with accounts of people who loved God and honored his Word.

In the race of life, there are many people cheering you on. Your friends and loved ones can encourage you when you are tired. You can also be inspired by the people who have gone before you. Read stories about people who faithfully followed Jesus and let them give you strength.

God, show me stories of people who have followed you. Thank you for the examples I have already seen.

APRIL 8

ALWAYS WELCOME

"Let the little children come to me."
MATTHEW 19:14 ICB

Jesus loves children. When everyone around him thought the children would bother him, Jesus welcomed them. He was never annoyed, impatient, or frustrated with children. He sees every child as precious, wonderful, and worthy of love.

Jesus adores you. You are so special to him. He is never too busy for you, and he is never annoyed by you. He wants you to know how much he loves you.

Jesus, thank you for always welcoming me into your presence. Hold me in your arms and show me how much you love me.

APRIL 9

GOD THE EXPERT

"My ways are higher than your ways.
My thoughts are higher than your thoughts."

ISAIAH 55:9 NIRV

Every good project starts with a plan. We can't build houses without knowing how to put together a wall, and we can't fix a car without knowing what each part is for. When we don't know how something works, we look for someone who does.

There is someone who can solve every problem you will ever face. God is an expert in everything. He is strong, smart, and he listens to you! No matter how stuck you feel, God can help.

> God, you are perfect at everything you do!
> Help me to run to you for help when I need it.

APRIL 10

BIGGER STORY

The LORD is the God who lives forever.
He created everything on earth.

ISAIAH 40:28 NIRV

It's easy to get caught up in our own lives. We focus on our problems and our victories. It's important to remember that we are part of a bigger story. There is more going on than what we can see with our eyes.

God created everything you see and more. He is bigger than you can imagine, and he will live forever. When you look beyond the details of your own day, you will see that God is at work in mighty ways.

God, help me see the story you've created.
Remind me that you are in control of everything.

APRIL 11

LISTEN

> My son, listen. Accept what I say.
> Then you will live for many years.
>
> PROVERBS 4:10 NIRV

We listen to God because he has proven that he is trustworthy. He is kind, and his love for us is unending. Everything he asks us to do is for our good. He is the very best leader, father, and friend.

It's important to listen to God. He loves you, and he knows what is best. If you pay attention, you will hear his voice. Just like you recognize your parents' voices, you will learn to recognize God's voice.

God, thank you for leading me.
Help me to hear your voice and obey.

APRIL 12

ALL THE CREDIT

> We are not able to claim anything for ourselves. The power
> to do what we do comes from God.
>
> 2 CORINTHIANS 3:5 NIRV

God deserves all the credit. We can do everything, from opening our eyes in the morning to finishing our homework, because of his strength. He gives us the power to live, breathe, and follow him.

Glorify God for everything he is doing. He holds the entire world together, and he keeps a watchful eye over you. He has woven your life together, and he makes sure that his will is accomplished.

> God, all the glory belongs to you!
> I praise you for all you are doing.

APRIL 13

A SON'S PRAYERS

> The prayer of a godly person is powerful. Things happen because of it.
>
> JAMES 5:16 NIRV

We don't have to say the perfect words for God to hear us. Our thoughts don't need to be perfectly organized, and our questions don't need to be just right. If we put our faith in Jesus and trust in God's promises, he will hear us.

Your prayers are powerful and strong. Just because you are young, it doesn't mean God hears you less. God hears every prayer even if you don't know what to say. He won't ever laugh at you.

God, I'm so glad I can talk to you. Thank you for hearing my prayers even when they aren't neat and tidy.

APRIL 14

LOVE OVER PRIDE

> Love is not jealous, it does not brag, and it is not proud.
>
> 1 CORINTHIANS 13:4 NCV

God is love. He is not jealous, and he does not brag. Even though he is completely perfect, he doesn't make us feel bad or like we aren't good enough. That's not how we should act either.

It's okay to be proud of yourself when you've worked hard at something. It's not okay to use that to make other people feel bad. If you want to love others well, don't brag about what you've done or what you have.

God, help me to stay quiet when I am tempted to brag. Fill my heart with love instead of pride.

APRIL 15

IN CONTROL

Trust in the Lord with all your heart.
Do not depend on your own understanding.

PROVERBS 3:5 NIRV

We can't see past the moment we are in. Even when we make the best plans, we still don't know what the future will bring. Anything can happen, and it's important to realize we aren't in control.

God sees what you can't see. He knows more about your life than you do. It makes sense to do what he says. He knows what each of your days will look like.

God, you know more than me. Help me to trust you.

APRIL 16

BEING AFRAID

"The Lord is with us.
Don't be afraid of them."
NUMBERS 14:9 NIRV

A big storm can cause fear to rise up. The first day of school can make you feel nervous. A movie might be too scary to watch. It is normal to feel fear. The important thing is how you react when you feel afraid.

God's love is big enough to handle all of your fears. His love can make you brave when you are afraid. Remember that God is on your side. He is with you, and he can give you peace.

God, thank you for being close when I am afraid. Help me to trust in your strength.

APRIL 17

SLOW TO ANGER

The Lord is gracious and compassionate,
slow to anger and rich in love.

PSALM 145:8 NIV

People are not perfect and don't always react the right way. Sometimes we let our emotions boil within us and explode from our mouths. We say things we shouldn't, or we forget how our actions make people feel.

God is slow to anger. He is not easily frustrated or annoyed. He does not roll his eyes at you or lose his patience. He is rich in compassion. This means that he cares for you, and he thinks about how you feel. No matter what, God's love for you will not change.

> God, help me to see how much you love me.
> Thank you for your perfect love.

APRIL 18

READY TO HELP

> Our help is in the name of the Lord,
> the Maker of heaven and earth.
>
> PSALM 124:8 NIV

If God is big enough to make the heavens and the earth, then he is big enough to help us with whatever we need. There is no problem that is too big for God. Our help comes from the God who can do anything!

Don't try to solve your problems all by yourself. You don't need to be strong. You don't need to prove that you can do it by yourself. The best solution is to ask God for help. No matter how big or small your problem is, God wants to help you.

*God, thank you for always helping me.
Teach me how to depend on you.*

APRIL 19

PEACE AND QUIET

He makes me lie down in green pastures,
He leads me beside quiet waters.

PSALM 23:2 NIV

God says that he leads us by quiet waters and green pastures. Doesn't that sound peaceful? No matter how crazy it feels on the outside, God can put peace in our hearts. He can help us breathe deeply and find a quiet place.

True peace comes from the inside, and it doesn't depend on how much noise there is on the outside. God is the only one who can give you true peace. Instead of trying to change what is going on around you, focus on asking God to give you peace.

God, thank you for taking care of me.
Help me depend on you for peace.

APRIL 20

GO AND TELL

"Go everywhere in the world, and tell the Good News to everyone."

MARK 16:15 NCV

Before he went back to heaven, Jesus told his disciples to tell the good news to everyone. He knew that people would need to hear about what he had done. He knew that learning about his death and resurrection would give people hope.

You can give hope to people by telling them about Jesus and by loving them like he does. There is no other solution to the hurt and pain you will see in the world. When you tell others about the love of Jesus, you give them a great gift.

God, thank you for giving me the gift of the gospel. Help me to share this gift with others.

APRIL 21

WELL DONE

> Pay careful attention to your own work, for then you will get the satisfaction of a job well done, and you won't need to compare yourself to anyone else. For we are each responsible for our own conduct.
>
> GALATIANS 6:4-5 NLT

A job well done can be really satisfying. When we have a task to do, we can honor God by doing our best. We are each responsible for what is in front of us. We don't need to compare our work to anyone else's.

Today, do your best with whatever work you have. If you've been asked to do the dishes, walk the dog, or finish your homework, do it well. Your hard work is worship to God.

God, I want to be the kind of person who works hard and does a good job.

APRIL 22

THE GOOD SHEPHERD

> The LORD is my shepherd;
> I have everything I need.
>
> PSALM 23:1 NCV

A shepherd makes sure that his sheep are well fed. He keeps them safe from predators. He rescues them from dangerous places. He keeps them healthy and makes sure they have water to drink. He knows what is best for them, and he gives them what they need.

This is exactly how God treats you. Just like a shepherd will never leave his sheep, God will never leave you. He will always make sure you are provided for. You are precious to him, and he loves to take care of you.

God, thank you for taking care of me and giving me what I need.

APRIL 23

PLANS AND MIRACLES

"This happened so the power of God could be seen in him."
JOHN 9:3 NLT

God could easily accomplish his plans without the help of people; he is strong enough to do it all alone. Even though he is capable, he wants people to be part of his plans. He loves to do miracles through his people so his power can be seen.

When you depend on God, he will do great things through you. He will use you to encourage others, heal the sick, and comfort the broken. He will use your life as a way of showing others how powerful and loving he is. He wants you to be on his team.

> God, thank you for all that you are doing.
> Show me how I can be part of your plans.

APRIL 24

STAY CLOSE

> "Remain in me, and I will remain in you. No branch can produce fruit alone. It must remain in the vine."
>
> JOHN 15:4 ICB

We all need God. He is our Creator, and true life comes only from him. We need to stay connected to him if we want to have fruitful lives. In other words, we aren't meant to figure everything out alone.

Stay close to God, and he will take care of you. Spend time with him and you will produce good fruit. Trying to get through life without him is like cutting yourself off from the best help you could ever be given.

God, keep me close to you. Thank you for giving me the help I need.

BE HUMBLE

God continues to give us more grace. That's why Scripture says, "God opposes those who are proud. But he gives grace to those who are humble."

JAMES 4:6 NIRV

Asking for help isn't always easy. Sometimes we just want to do something on our own. It's not wrong to be independent, but it is wrong to be prideful. No matter how strong we are, we should always be willing to ask for help.

When you ask for help, you admit you cannot do it alone. This is called *humility*. God promises to always help those who are humble. He cannot help someone who is prideful because they don't even realize they need help.

God, I don't want to be prideful. Help me to learn humility. Teach me how to ask you for help.

APRIL 26

MATURE

> The whole body depends on Christ. And all the parts of the body are joined and held together. Each part of the body does its own work. And this makes the whole body grow and be strong with love.
>
> EPHESIANS 4:16 ICB

When we are young, we sometimes get tired of being told what to do. We imagine making our own decisions, and we look forward to having freedom. Being grown up sounds so exciting.

The truth is, we all need each other. As your responsibility grows, you'll actually need the people around you even more. It's important to support and teach each other with love and kindness no matter how old you get.

God, remind me how much I need the people around me. Teach me how to encourage my family and friends.

APRIL 27

BUILD UP

Let us do all we can to live in peace. And let us work hard to build up one another.

Romans 14:19 NIrV

We don't always feel like being kind to each other. Sometimes we lose our patience, or we let don't control our tempers. No matter how we feel, we can use our actions to build others up. We get to decide how we will behave.

Peace takes work. Treating each other with kindness takes practice. The more you pay attention to loving others well, the more you will improve. If you are struggling with one person, try asking God to change your heart. He loves teaching his children how to love each other.

God, teach me how to live in peace. I want to build people up with my words and actions.

APRIL 28

STEADFAST

He won't be afraid of bad news.
He is safe because he trusts the Lord.

PSALM 112:7 ICB

The Bible never promises that life will be easy. Following Jesus doesn't mean that we won't experience difficult things. We all have obstacles to overcome. Even so, we don't have to be afraid of the future.

God promises that your faith in him will bring you comfort and security no matter what you face. Even when life doesn't go the way you want, you can remain steadfast in Jesus. When you are sad, afraid, or worried, you can trust that God never changes, and he is by your side.

God, teach me how to be steadfast. I want to trust you even when life is hard.

APRIL 29

BE AWARE

> Stay alert! Watch out for your great enemy, the devil. He prowls around like a roaring lion, looking for someone to devour.
>
> 1 PETER 5:8 NLT

Satan's greatest goal is to separate you from God. He doesn't want you to trust God or believe his promises. He loves to distract you from the truth and cause you to doubt God's goodness. He wants you to think that God cannot or will not help you.

Pay attention to anything that causes you to turn away from God. Remember that no matter how far you might feel from God, there is nothing big enough to keep you from his love.

God, help me to trust in your goodness always.

APRIL 30

ETERNAL WORD

"The grass dies, and the flowers fall.
But the word of our God will live forever."

ISAIAH 40:8 ICB

God's Word is the only thing that will last forever. Everything about our lives will fade away. When our days are done, we cannot take anything with us. All of the treasures we've stored up on earth will eventually become trash.

When you store God's Word in your heart, you are collecting something that will never fade. You are gathering treasures that will never be taken away from you. His Word is more valuable than anything.

God, help me store your Word in my heart.
Help me memorize it and pay attention to it.

MAY

"I will make you strong
and will help you.
I will support you with
my right hand that saves you."

Isaiah 41:10 ICB

SHOWING KINDNESS

You know that Christ was rich, but for you he became poor so that by his becoming poor you might become rich.

2 CORINTHIANS 8:9 NCV

Jesus gave up everything to save us. He knew that we would be lost without him. He knew how important it was for us to be close to God, so he gave up all of his riches and comfort.

Jesus did not die on the cross as God. He died as a man. It didn't hurt less because he is God's Son. He suffered in the same way you would. His sacrifice is worthy of all your praise. He gave his life so that you could live forever.

*Jesus, thank you for your sacrifice!
I can never thank you enough.*

MAY 2

FULL OF LOVE

> Satisfy us in the morning with your unfailing love,
> that we may sing for joy and be glad all our days.
>
> PSALM 90:14 NIV

God's love can fill us up to the brim. Just when we think we have had enough, he gives us even more. There is no limit to his love. He will never run out, and he will never get tired of caring for his children.

Does God's love make you sing for joy and fill you with happiness? It brings him great joy to shower you with his love. He wants you to know how precious you are to him. You can never ask for too much of God's love.

*God, fill my heart with your love.
I want to be joyful all of my days.*

MAY 3

GIFT OF WORSHIP

> Honor the LORD for the glory of his name.
> Worship the LORD in the splendor of his holiness.
>
> PSALM 29:2 NLT

Gifts are such a treat. It's fun to get a present especially when we aren't expecting it. We feel noticed, loved, and cared for when someone takes the time to do something special for us.

Worship is your gift to God. When you take the time to honor his name with words, songs, or actions, he feels loved. When you thank him for what he's done and trust in his promises, you offer him a wonderful present.

> God, today I want to say that I love you.
> I am so thankful for all you have done for me.

MAY 4

DO WELL

> May my friends sing and shout for joy.
> May they always say, "Praise the greatness of the Lord.
> He loves to see his servants do well."
>
> PSALM 35:27 ICB

God loves to see his servants do well. He is not a mean or strict father who is waiting for us to mess up. He is not angrily watching us with a list of rules in his hands. He is a kind and loving father who wants the very best for his children.

Do you know that God looks at you with love and gentleness? He wants you to do well. He does not want you to be stressed out or feel like nothing you do is good enough. Praise him because he is the very best father there is.

God, you make me shout with joy! Thank you for wanting what's best for me.

MAY 5

ALL DAY

> The Lord's name should be praised
> from where the sun rises to where it sets.
>
> PSALM 113:3 ICB

The Bible says to praise God from the rising to the setting sun. This means that our day should be filled with praise from beginning to end. Every moment is an opportunity to honor God's name. There are so many reasons to thank him.

From the moment your eyes open, you can praise God. Tell him the things you love about him and thank him for the blessings in life. If you pay attention, you will find endless reasons to thank him.

God, help me thank you all day long. Help me to see all the wonderful things you have done.

MAY 6

NO DARKNESS

God is light; in him there is no darkness at all.

1 JOHN 1:5 NIV

When it is dark, we look for light. We automatically try to see the best we can. We look for a switch to turn on, a curtain to open, or we focus our eyes to try and navigate the dark. We do not naturally feel safe in the dark.

God is pure light. With him, you can overcome any darkness you face. He can light up every corner of your life with his love and kindness. When you cannot see what is in front of you, he will help you. When you feel lost, he will guide you.

God, thank you for your light. Fill my heart with your love and help me follow you.

MAY 7

GOD KNOWS

He gives strength to those who are tired.
He gives power to those who are weak.

ISAIAH 40:29 NIRV

When we are tired, it is good to ask for help. God has everything we need! There is no one better to run to when we are weary, weak, or overwhelmed. He made each of us and he knows exactly how to help.

God created you and he knows you inside and out. When something isn't right, he knows exactly how to make it better. He is the only one who can give you the strength you need when you are weak.

God, you know me better than anyone. Remind me to run to you for strength when I am weak.

MAY 8

KEPT SAFE

> During danger he will keep me safe in his shelter.
> He will hide me in his Holy Tent.
> Or he will keep me safe on a high mountain.
>
> PSALM 27:5-6 ICB

God sees each of us, and he knows how to keep us safe. He knows exactly who needs protection, and he has what it takes to provide it. He is big enough and strong enough to watch over each of his children. There is nothing greater than God.

Any enemy you face cannot compare to God. There is no situation too scary or risky for him. He is capable of protecting you no matter what. Even when something seems terrifying or impossible to you, God is not afraid.

God, thank you for keeping me safe. Thank you for protecting me even when I don't realize you are.

MAY 9

ALL TOGETHER

> Then I looked, and there was a great number of people.
> There were so many people that no one could count them.
> They were from every nation, tribe, people,
> and language of the earth.
>
> REVELATION 7:9 ICB

In the book of Revelation, John describes his vision of heaven. He sees every person who has ever put their faith in God worshipping at the feet of Jesus. There are more people than he can count! Heaven will be filled with people from all parts of the earth.

One day everyone will worship God together. It won't matter what language you speak or what color your skin is. We will all be united in our love for Jesus no matter how different we are. It will be a glorious day!

God, I'm excited to worship you with people from all over the earth!

MAY 10

NO SECRETS

He knows what is in our hearts.

PSALM 44:21 ICB

We've all stretched the truth at some point. We know it's wrong to lie, but it's tempting to do the wrong thing if we think we can get away with it.

You can't hide things from God. He sees what is in your heart, and he knows what is best for you. When he tells you something is wrong, don't be afraid. Confess what you've done and let God's love change your heart.

God, you are gentle and kind, and I want to honor you with my actions, thoughts, and words.

MAY 11

FAITH

Without faith no one can please God.

HEBREWS 11:6 ICB

Faith means believing in something that cannot be seen. It's like knowing the sun is still there even when it's cloudy. Just because we cannot see it doesn't mean we wonder if it will ever be sunny again.

The same thing is true about your faith in God. Even on days when you cannot feel him, you can trust that he is still there. He has promised that he will never leave you. The more you believe in him, the stronger your faith will become.

God, please make my faith stronger. When I am doubtful, remind me that you will never leave me.

MAY 12

DO GOOD

Wisdom that comes from God is like this: First, it is pure. Then it is also peaceful, gentle, and easy to please. This wisdom is always ready to help those who are troubled and to do good for others.

JAMES 3:17 ICB

When we think of wisdom, we might think about being really smart or having all the right answers. It's important to look at wisdom the way God does instead of using our own definition. Godly wisdom is peaceful and always ready to help others.

Having wisdom isn't about being smart or right all the time. You show that you are wise when you are kind and willing to do good for others.

God, please give me wisdom. Show me how I can help people who are in trouble.

MAY 13

GREAT THINGS

"He who believes in me will do the same things that I do."

JOHN 14:12 ICB

Jesus did amazing things in his life. He raised the dead. He healed the sick. He made the lonely feel welcome. Jesus said that if we believe in him, we can do these things too.

You have the same power in you that Jesus had. You have the same access to God and all of his resources. Don't be afraid to ask him for big things just like Jesus.

> God, thank you for the example of Jesus.
> Help me to have faith just like him.

MAY 14

KNOW HIS LOVE

> Lord, your love reaches to the heavens.
> Your loyalty goes to the skies.
>
> PSALM 36:5 ICB

God's love is higher than the sky and bigger than outer space. It doesn't have any limits, and it will never end. We could spend all day everyday learning about God's love, and we would never know it all.

God's love can give you hope, and it can change your heart. His love can take you from sadness to joy and from anger to peace. No matter what is going on in your life, God's love can make a difference.

God, help me to understand how much you love me.

MAY 15

THANKFUL HEART

> This is the day the LORD has made.
> Let us rejoice and be glad today!
>
> PSALM 118:24 NCV

Each day is God's creation. He has woven each moment together. When things don't look the way we want, it's good to remember that God is the author of our days. He is the one in control.

It is good for your heart to be thankful for each day you are given. Thankfulness keeps your heart from being bitter or negative. Thank God for the day he has given you today.

God, thank you for today! Thank you for the gifts you have given me and for leading me so well.

MAY 16

ALWAYS PRESENT

> God is our refuge and strength,
> an ever-present help in trouble.
>
> PSALM 46:1 NIV

People can't always help us, but God is our ever-present help. That means he is always available. We can always count on him. He will not let us down, and he will not ignore our cries for help.

God is on your side! He is your helper, and he wants to give you strength. If you let him, he will guide you through every trial and problem you face. No matter how impossible something seems, God can see you through.

God, I am so thankful for your help! Teach me how to run to you first when problems come up.

MAY 17

FORGIVENESS

> "When you offer your gift to God at the altar, and you remember that your brother or sister has something against you, leave your gift there at the altar. Go and make peace with that person, and then come and offer your gift."
>
> MATTHEW 5:23-24 NCV

God reminds us to forgive others because he knows that staying upset isn't good for our hearts. He says to forgive others because he has forgiven us. We can show God's love to other people when we forgive like he does.

God wants you to have peace with others. He doesn't want you to hold onto hurt, and he doesn't want you to be unaware of how you've hurt others. When you do the wrong thing, apologize and ask for forgiveness.

God, thank you for teaching me how to forgive. Help me to make peace with those around me.

MAY 18

LOVE ONE ANOTHER

Let us continue to love one another, for love comes from God. Anyone who loves is a child of God and knows God. But anyone who does not love does not know God, for God is love.

1 JOHN 4:7-8 NLT

When we love others well, we show that we are God's children. Love comes from God, and we cannot display true love without reflecting who he is. If we pay attention, we will notice many opportunities to love other people.

You can love your friends and family by thinking about what they need. You love like Jesus when you set aside what you want to focus on someone else.

God, help me show your love to the people around me. Help me put the needs of others before my own.

MAY 19

BE BOLD

> Let us come boldly to the throne of our gracious God. There we will receive his mercy, and we will find grace to help us when we need it most.
>
> HEBREWS 4:16 NLT

God never changes, and he always keeps his promises. If he says that he will give us mercy, then he will always give us mercy. We don't have to be nervous to be honest with God.

Have you ever done something wrong and been afraid to admit it? You might be worried about what will be said to you or what the consequence will be. You don't have to be afraid to approach God. You can tell him your biggest mistake or your deepest secret, and he will always give you mercy.

God, thank you for letting me talk to you boldly. When I make a mistake, help me to turn to you quickly.

MAY 20

PRAISE GOD

> Clap your hands, all you people.
> Shout to God with joy.
> The Lord Most High is wonderful.
> He is the great King over all the earth!
>
> Psalm 47:1-2 NCV

There is always something we can be thankful for. Having an attitude of gratitude creates joy. This is because the more we pay attention to what we have, the less we will feel jealous or upset about what we don't have.

Pay close attention to all that God has given you. Praise him for all he has done. Tell him all the things you love about him. He is a great King and the best Father. He is wonderful, mighty, and kind. There will never be enough words to describe the goodness of God.

*God, thank you for all you have done.
Thank you for all you have given me.*

GOD'S WISDOM

> Don't depend on your own wisdom.
> Respect the LORD and refuse to do wrong.
>
> PROVERBS 3:7 NCV

Even if we know a lot, we still don't know as much as God. It doesn't make sense to insist on our own way when we have God on our side. We don't need all the answers because God has them.

You can always depend on God's knowledge. It doesn't have an end! There isn't anything he doesn't know. No matter what problem you have, God can help you solve it.

God, your wisdom is so much greater than mine. Remind me to depend on you!

MAY 22

GOD KNOWS YOU

> O LORD, you have examined my heart
> and know everything about me.
>
> PSALM 139:1 NLT

We don't have to be on our best behavior with God because he already sees everything. We cannot hide anything from him, and there is nowhere we can go to escape his love. He sees us, understands us, and loves us fully.

God knows you better than anyone. Your mom and dad probably know you better than anyone on earth, but that still doesn't compare to how deeply God knows you. There is nothing about you that he doesn't understand, and there is nothing about you that surprises him.

God, thank for knowing me perfectly. Thank you for loving me and for always understanding me.

MAY 23

WHAT GOD WANTS

What does the Lord require of you?
To act justly and to love mercy
and to walk humbly with your God.

Micah 6:8 niv

We all have times when we aren't sure what to do. We want to make good choices, but we don't always know what that looks like. It's important to remember that we can find answers in the Bible.

God's Word says to act justly, love mercy, and walk humbly. This means that you do what is right or fair, you think about others first, and you know that you need God. When you don't know what to do, start with those things.

God, thank you for your Word. Help me to act justly, love mercy, and walk humbly with you.

MAY 24

LIFT UP

People enjoy giving good answers!
Saying the right word at the right time is so pleasing!

PROVERBS 15:23 ICB

It's important to pay attention to what you say. Your words can have a big impact. You can either lift up others or tear them down. We are each in control of our tongues, and we get to decide how we treat the people around us.

What you say matters. You are the only one who can control what comes out of your mouth. When you are careless with your words, you can hurt people's feelings. Instead, bring life with what you say.

God, help me use my words to love others.

MAY 25

PRIDE

"Don't continue bragging.
Don't speak proud words.
The Lord is a God who knows everything.
He judges what people do."

1 Samuel 2:3 NIV

When we brag about something we've done, it's usually because we want to be noticed. We like it when other people think good things about us. It's not wrong to be proud of our actions, but it is important to value God's opinion over the opinions of other people.

There is no need to brag about your accomplishments. God knows all you have done, and he will be faithful to reward you. You don't have to look for your own rewards.

God, thank you for seeing everything. Help me to trust in your opinion above all others.

MAY 26

ENDURANCE

> Patient endurance is what you need now,
> so that you will continue to do God's will.
> Then you will receive all that he has promised.
>
> HEBREWS 10:36 NLT

It's always worth it to build up our endurance. When we have endurance, we are able to keep going even when we don't want to. Every good thing in our lives requires endurance.

It would be nice if you could skip the challenging parts of life but that isn't realistic. Some difficulties cannot be avoided. When challenges come up, don't be discouraged! Ask God to give you endurance, and he will walk with you through whatever you are facing.

God, teach me how to endure instead of quitting. Give me strength when I am tired.

MAY 27

IN CONFIDENCE

The words of a gossip are like tasty bits of food.
People take them all in.

PROVERBS 18:8 ICB

Gossiping is when we share information that isn't ours to tell. We don't need to know everything about everyone. Some things should be kept to ourselves. It can be fun to talk about other people, but it doesn't result in anything good.

If a friend tells you something about their life, they probably told it to you in secret. This means they shared it thinking you would keep it to yourself. People will trust you when they see that you can treat their stories with care.

God, teach me how to be a good friend. Help me keep my mouth shut when I am tempted to gossip.

MAY 28

ENOUGH

"You must not covet your neighbor's house…
or anything else that belongs to your neighbor."

EXODUS 20:17 NLT

Coveting means wanting something that doesn't belong to us; it's a lot like jealousy. When we covet what other people have, we will quickly become unhappy with our own things.

If you feel stuck in jealousy, ask God to help you. He will show you the blessings you have, and he will remind you of his love for you. He wants your heart to be at peace instead of being anxious and full of jealousy.

God, forgive me for the times I've been jealous of others. Help me to focus on the blessings I have.

MAY 29

HE WON'T FAIL

> I wait patiently for God to save me.
> Only he gives me hope.
>
> PSALM 62:5 ICB

God never fails. Everything he sets out to do gets done perfectly. If he makes a promise, we can trust him to accomplish it. If he designs a plan, we know that it will happen.

Following God isn't always easy, but he will not disappoint you. Life will have challenges, but God will not let you down. He will be with you through it all. God is close to you on your best and worst days.

God, all of my hope is in you! Thank you for being reliable and strong.

MAY 30

BE CURIOUS

> He has made everything beautiful in its time. He has also given people a sense of who he is. But they can't completely understand what God has done from beginning to end.
>
> ECCLESIASTES 3:11 NIRV

God is greater than we can understand. Everything about him is perfect and wonderful. We can grasp parts of who he is, but our human minds cannot understand him fully. He is more incredible and amazing than we can know.

You could read the whole Bible, and you still wouldn't fully understand God. Until you meet him face-to-face, there will always be parts of him that are beyond you. This is not supposed to be bad news. It means you can never run out of things to explore!

God, give me curiosity about who you are. Help me spend all my life learning about you.

MAY 31

ANY STORM

> Through our faith, Christ has brought us into that blessing of God's grace that we now enjoy. And we are happy because of the hope we have of sharing God's glory.
>
> ROMANS 5:2 ICB

God said Jesus would come back again and make all things right. Reminding ourselves of his promises can bring strength when life is hard. Looking forward to seeing God's glory can help us stay strong when difficult things happen.

When you decide to follow Jesus, you put your faith in him. You believe that he is the Son of God, his death redeemed you, and he is coming back again. If you hold to these truths, you can make it through any storm.

God, help me remember your truth when life is hard.

JUNE 1

NEW LIFE

> You were taught to start living a new life. It is created to be truly good and holy, just as God is.
>
> EPHESIANS 4:24 NIRV

When we have a job to do, the first step is making sure we have the right tools. If we are building a snowman, we need clothes to keep us warm. If we are baking cookies we need to have the right ingredients. We can't move forward with any task if we don't have what we need.

When you choose to follow God, he gives you everything you need. You already have the right tools for the job. God has given you a new life, and he has made sure you are not missing anything.

God, thank you for helping me follow you. Teach me how to worship you in all I do.

JUNE 2

LOYAL AND STEADY

The Lord is faithful; he will strengthen you and guard you from the evil one.

2 THESSALONIANS 3:3 NLT

Someone who is faithful is loyal and steady. A faithful friend doesn't give up when life gets hard. A faithful dog stays close when danger is near. Being faithful means being there no matter what.

God is always faithful; he is strong and steady. Even if the mountains crumble, he will not change. His love for you cannot be taken away. When you put your trust in him, he will strengthen you and protect you.

God, I feel stronger knowing that you are right by my side. Thank you for being faithful to me.

JUNE 3

GREAT HELPER

> Lord, you do everything for me.
> Lord, your love continues forever.
> You made us. Do not leave us.
>
> PSALM 138:8 ICB

Life would be impossible if we had to do everything by ourselves. We all need help in big and small ways. Through every stage of your life, God is your great helper. He is on your side, and he has everything you need.

No matter what problems come up, God is capable and strong. He created you, and he will not leave you. Put your trust in him, and he will walk with you for your whole life.

God, thank you for always helping me.

JUNE 4

UNENDING LOVE

> Praise the Lord!
> Thank the Lord because he is good.
> His love continues forever.
>
> PSALM 106:1 ICB

God never gets tired of us. He doesn't get fed up with our sins, and he isn't annoyed by our constant needs. He loves to take care of us. We are his favorite part of creation!

God's love for you is great. It will never change or fade away. You don't ever have to worry about being left or ignored. You don't have to be afraid that he is mad at you. God is good all the time, and his love for you cannot be measured.

> God, thank you for your unending love.
> Help me to be confident in you.

JUNE 5

EXACTLY ALIKE

> The Son reflects the glory of God. He is an exact copy of God's nature.
>
> HEBREWS 1:3 ICB

Jesus is a perfect reflection of God the Father. We don't have to wonder what God is like because we can look at Jesus. We can read about the way he acted and the things he said.

If you want to know more about God, learn about Jesus. If you want to know how God acts, look at Jesus. God is not a mystery because he sent his Son to show you what he is like.

God, thank you for sending Jesus to be the way to you. Teach me more about who you are.

JUNE 6

GOD'S CREATIVITY

> The heavens tell the glory of God.
> And the skies announce what his hands have made.
> Day after day they tell the story.
> Night after night they tell it again.
>
> PSALM 19:1-2 ICB

Amazing beauty is all around us. It's easy to get used to it and take it for granted. When we see something every day, we might forget that it's a miracle. It's important to take time to notice God's creativity.

Study a flower. Sit and watch the sun rise or set. Write down some dreams and remember that God loves to do beautiful things. He is very creative, and everything he does is glorious. He will make your life beautiful as well.

God, you are truly awesome.
The world you have made is beautiful.

JUNE 7

WHAT IS NEXT

Show me the right path, O Lord;
point out the road for me to follow.

PSALM 25:4 NLT

God is the best teacher, and he will show us the right steps one at a time. He will lead the way, so we don't need to worry. We can relax and follow him because he has everything under control.

There will be so many choices to make as you grow up. Some of them are small like what color backpack to get for school. Others will be big like what college to go to, or what job to look for. If you let him, God will help you with every decision you make.

God, thank you for being a perfect leader.
Help me make decisions that honor you.

JUNE 8

KNIT TOGETHER

"Before I formed you in your mother's body I chose you.
Before you were born I set you apart to serve me.
I appointed you to be a prophet to the nations."

JEREMIAH 1:5 NIRV

It's amazing to think that God knew us before we were born. He saw all of our days clearly before we even lived one of them. Our lives have been perfectly planned by the same God who placed the sun and stars in the sky.

Your parents love you just because you belong to them. Imagine how much more God loves you simply because you belong to him. He has great things planned for your life.

God, when I feel small, remind me I am yours. Thank you for giving me life.

WEAK AND STRONG

> "When you are weak,
> my power is made perfect in you."
>
> 2 Corinthians 12:9 NCV

We don't like to feel helpless. When we have a job to do, we want to feel strong and able. It's important to remember that God's strength is more important than our own. No matter what problem we are facing, God is big enough to handle it.

God is stronger than you are. When you are weak and tired, God can show you just how strong he is. You don't have to be embarrassed that you can't do something on your own. God is always ready to help you.

God, you are always stronger than I am!
Remind me to ask you for help when I feel weak.

JUNE 10

LOVE AS GOD LOVES

If God loved us that much we also should love each other.

1 JOHN 4:11 NCV

There are so many ways we can love each other. We can share our favorite things, be ready to help, and be encouraging and kind with our words. Loving the people around us doesn't happen by accident. We need to love people on purpose.

It makes God happy when you love others. He loves you so much, and he wants you to treat others the same way he treats you. He cares for you, so you care for others.

> God, thank you for loving me so much. Help me to love the people around me in the same way.

JUNE 11

TAKEN CARE OF

> "I tell you, do not worry about your life, what you will eat; or about your body, what you will wear."
>
> LUKE 12:22 NIV

Jesus can take care of all our needs. There is nothing we need to worry about. He is a kind father who wants to take care of his children. He isn't bothered or annoyed when we ask for things.

You are loved and protected by God. He is strong enough to take care of you. If you let him, he can take your worries and replace them with peace. Tell him what you need and trust that he can handle it.

God, thank you for giving me what I need. Help me to trust in you more each day.

JUNE 12

PIECE BY PIECE

You made my whole being;
you formed me in my mother's body.

PSALM 139:13 NCV

Imagine building a house, painting a masterpiece, or putting together a robot. Few of us can do those things, even if someone shows us how. Even with step-by-step instructions, those are complicated tasks to master.

Your body is more complex than anything humans can make. God is the only one who can create life. He carefully puts each piece together exactly how it belongs. He lovingly made you with great attention to detail.

God, thank you for the way you made me.
You are a wise and kind creator.

JUNE 13

ALONG THE WAY

Remember your leaders who taught God's message to you.
HEBREWS 13:7 NCV

We all have someone in our lives who has taught us about God. Whether it's a parent, teacher, or neighbor, someone has shared God's goodness with us. We cannot follow God alone, and it's important to remember the people who have helped us along the way.

God puts people in your life for a reason. If you pay attention, you can learn something from the people around you.

> God, thank you for the people in my life who have taught me about you.

JUNE 14

GOOD FRIENDS

Godly people are careful about the friends they choose. But the way of sinners leads them down the wrong path.

PROVERBS 12:26 NIRV

Friends can have a huge impact on our lives. If we have good friends, they can support us and cause us to grow closer to God. If we have bad friends, they can impact us in negative ways and bring us down.

Choose your friends carefully. A solid friend who makes good choices is more important than having a friend because you want to fit in. It takes courage to make wise choices with your friendships. Ask God for help, and he will strengthen you to do it.

God, please protect my friendships. Help me make wise decisions so I can stay on the right path.

JUNE 15

KINDNESS ALWAYS

Do not do wrong to repay a wrong, and do not insult to repay an insult. But repay with a blessing, because you yourselves were called to do this so that you might receive a blessing.

1 PETER 3:9 NCV

When someone is hurtful, it's really tempting to hurt them back. This isn't how the Bible tells us to live. Instead of using our words or actions to get revenge, we are supposed to repay hurt with blessings.

It's not always easy to do the right thing, but God promises to reward you. When you are kind to someone who hurts you, you love like God loves. It honors him when you bless others.

God, teach me to control my words when I am hurt or angry. Help me to love others like you do.

JUNE 16

TELL HIM EVERYTHING

> No matter what happens, tell God about everything.
> Ask and pray, and give thanks to him.
>
> PHILIPPIANS 4:6 NIRV

God is our gentle father, mighty king, wise teacher, and trusted friend. We can talk to God and tell him everything. There is nothing we need to hide from God. He wants us to talk with him about the big and small things in our lives.

When you wake up in the morning, talk to God. When you are eating breakfast, talk to God. When you are at school, talk to God. Every moment is a good moment to pray and give thanks to him for all he has done.

God, teach me how to talk to you all the time.

JUNE 17

JOYFUL AND CONTENT

I can do everything through Christ, who gives me strength.

PHILIPPIANS 4:13 NLT

When Paul said this, he was talking about being content. When we are content, we are satisfied with what we have. We aren't always wishing for more things or for life to be different. We trust God no matter what is happening around us.

God can do big things! He can teach you how to be content even when everyone around you isn't. You can be joyful and full of peace even when life doesn't look exactly how you want. God will give you strength in every situation.

God, thank you for giving me strength.
Teach me how to be content.

JUNE 18

TO LOVE GOD

> "I tell you the truth, anything you did for even the least of my people here, you also did for me."
>
> MATTHEW 25:40 NCV

One of the most important things God asks us to do is love others. His first commandment is to love him, and his second is to love those around us. He doesn't give us a long list of rules or requirements, but he does ask us to treat other people with kindness and love.

When you show love for others, you are showing love for God. When you share with your friend, it is like you are sharing with God. When you help your parents with chores, it is like you are helping God. The most important thing you can do is love others.

God, I am glad that I can love you by loving others.

JUNE 19

THE CLAY

> Yet, O Lord, you are our Father.
> We are the clay, you are the potter;
> we are all the work of your hand.
>
> Isaiah 64:8 niv

God is our Creator. He is like a potter who makes vases and bowls out of clay. We are the clay, and he has formed each of us carefully. When a potter molds clay, the clay doesn't tell him what to do or point out mistakes. The clay simply does what the potter wants.

In the same way, it isn't your job to focus on your flaws. God is the one who made you, and he does not make mistakes. You are wonderfully and carefully made. When he looks at you, he doesn't see problems or imperfections. You are his son, and he is proud of you.

God, help me to focus on how you see me.
Thank you for the way you made me.

JUNE 20

GOD AMONG US

> The Word became human and made his home among us. He was full of unfailing love and faithfulness.
>
> JOHN 1:14 NLT

God sent his Son, Jesus, to save us. He knew that we would need someone we could see with our own eyes and touch with our own hands. When Jesus came to earth, we received the best gift ever.

If you want to understand God, you can look at Jesus. Read about his life and pay attention to the way he loved people. When he walked the earth, he showed us exactly what God is like. His love for others teaches us about God's love.

God, thank you for sending Jesus to teach us about you.

JUNE 21

ON YOUR GUARD

Be on your guard; stand firm in the faith; be courageous; be strong. Do everything in love.

1 CORINTHIANS 16:13-14 NIV

God has given us the Holy Spirit to teach us how to live. He will often speak by nudging our hearts. That little feeling that maybe we are making the wrong choice is the Holy Spirit trying to warn us. He speaks quietly and gently if we are willing to listen.

As you get older, there will be plenty of opportunities to make the wrong choice. There will be times when your friends do something you know is wrong. You can either join them or you can stand up for what you know is right. It is important to be on your guard and listen to the Holy Spirit.

God, thank you for the voice of the Holy Spirit in my life. Teach me how to listen and follow what he says.

JUNE 22

BIG ENOUGH

> Trust God all the time.
> Tell him all your problems,
> because God is our protection.
>
> PSALM 62:8 NCV

Sometimes worry takes over our thoughts. When we focus on our fears, the same thoughts keep running through our heads. We become stressed out and might forget that God is near and ready to help us.

Take your worries and hand them to God. Tell him about your fears, and he will teach you how to trust him. When you give him your worries, he will give you peace. His peace will protect you and help you to stay calm.

God, thank you for being big enough to handle all my worries. I trust you with my fears.

JUNE 23

GREAT LOVE

> As high as the heavens are above the earth,
> so great is his love for those who fear him.
>
> PSALM 103:11 NIV

The United States is almost 3,000 miles long. By plane, it takes between six and seven hours to cross it. By car it takes between four and five days. If we walked, it could take six months! It can be hard to understand something that goes further than our eyes can see.

The Bible says that God's love for you is even bigger than those distances. It stretches further than anything you can imagine. You can try to picture it or make sense of it, but it is too big for that. His love for you is extraordinary.

God, thank you for your great love.

JUNE 24

FAITH

> Faith means being sure of the things we hope for. And faith means knowing that something is real even if we do not see it.
>
> HEBREWS 11:1 ICB

Even when we know God is real, we sometimes struggle to believe it. We might feel far away from him, or there might be things about God we don't understand. Even when we doubt, we can trust God to strengthen our faith.

It can be hard to think about God when he isn't right in front of you. This doesn't make you a bad Christian. God knew following him wouldn't always be easy. That's why he sent the Holy Spirit to guide you. The more you walk with him, the stronger your faith will get.

God, I want to have strong faith! Help me to trust in you even when I have doubts.

JUNE 25

LEGACY

> We will not hide these truths from our children;
> we will tell the next generation
> about the glorious deeds of the LORD,
> about his power and his mighty wonders.
>
> PSALM 78:4 NLT

God loves families. He loves it when parents teach their children about who he is. He wants us to pass down stories about his goodness and faithfulness. When we tell our children the truth, they will their children and so on. Each generation hears about what God has done from the people who came before them.

Maybe you didn't learn about God from your mom or dad, but whoever gave you this book was passing down truth to you because they love you. As we share God's love, his kingdom grows.

God, thank you for the truth I've been told about you. Help me to pass down stories of your faithfulness.

JUNE 26

MEANINGFUL

> I am as happy over your promises
> as if I had found a great treasure.
>
> PSALM 119:162 ICB

We all like to treasure hunt in different ways. Some of us like to search the library for our next great read. Some of us like to comb the beach for unique shells. No matter the details, when we find our treasure, we are delighted!

The Word of God is a treasure anyone can find. Every single thing God has said to you is meaningful and valuable. His Word is full of goodness. If you ask him, the Holy Spirit will show you wonderful things in the Word of God.

God, thank you for the treasure of your Word. Teach me how to understand it better.

JUNE 27

REWARDS

> We must not become tired of doing good. We will receive our harvest of eternal life at the right time. We must not give up!
>
> GALATIANS 6:9 ICB

Hard work always has rewards. When we finish our homework, we are rewarded with good grades. When we do our chores without complaining, we might be rewarded with the thankfulness of our parents.

Working hard for God also comes with rewards. God sees you persevering. He knows that following him is hard sometimes. If you do not give up, he will reward you.

God, give me strength when I am tired of doing the right thing. Thank you for promising to reward me with eternal life.

JUNE 28

CLEAR MEMORY

Love does not remember wrongs done against it.

1 CORINTHIANS 13:5 ICB

The Bible says that when we love someone, we shouldn't keep track of their mistakes. It's not kind to keep a list of someone's wrongs. We want our sins to be forgiven, so we should forgive others.

It's not always easy to forgive, but God will give you strength to do it. Through Christ you can love others the way God does. When someone does something wrong, don't keep a record of it or hold it against them.

God, you have forgiven me, and I want to forgive others. Help me keep my memory clear and full of love.

PART OF THE FAMILY

> If we are God's children, then we will receive the blessings God has for us.
>
> Romans 8:17 ICB

When our parents own something, we usually get to enjoy it. We live in their houses, eat their food, and use their things. If our parents own a boat, a vast library, or beautiful backyard, we get to enjoy it. Families share what they have.

You are part of a family much larger than you might know. As a follower of Jesus, you have been adopted into God's family. As a child of God, you get to share all of his treasures and resources. You have access to all of the goodness God has to offer.

God, thank you for sharing everything you have with me!

JUNE 30

ALWAYS MERCIFUL

> God has great mercy, and because of his mercy he gave us new life. He gave us a living hope because Jesus Christ rose from death.
>
> 1 PETER 1:3 ICB

God is merciful all the time. This means that he is kind to us when we don't deserve it. He gives us good gifts just because we are his children. We don't have to work harder to make him love us more. He loves us simply because we belong to him.

If you have put your trust in Jesus, God has given you extravagant mercy. He has taken your sin and made your heart clean. Even though you make mistakes and do the wrong thing, God has covered you with his love.

God, help me understand how merciful you are. Thank you for the way you love me.

JULY

The Lord defends those who suffer. He protects them in times of trouble.

Psalm 9:9 ICB

JULY 1

EVERY PROBLEM

> The LORD makes secure the footsteps
> of the person who delights in him,
> Even if that person trips, he won't fall.
> The LORD's hand takes good care of him.
>
> PSALM 37:23-24 NIRV

Life is full of ups and downs. Sometimes we make mistakes and have to deal with the consequences of our actions, and sometimes difficult things happen with no explanation. Either way, God promises to take care of us when we choose him.

You might not have faced many challenges yet, but you probably know life isn't always easy. The good news is that no matter what happens, God is on your side. If you trust in him, he will keep you steady.

*God, thank you for staying close to me.
Teach me how to walk through each problem I face.*

JULY 2

SHOW LOVE

"All people will know that you are my followers
if you love each other."

JOHN 13:35 NCV

As we learn more about God, we realize that we are supposed to share his goodness with others. This might feel like a big, scary, task. We might imagine boldly declaring God's truth to everyone who will listen.

God said that if your actions are loving, people will notice. The way you treat others means more than anything else. When you are kind, thoughtful, helpful, and a peacemaker, you show that you belong to God.

God, teach me to love like you so I can show your love to those around me.

JULY 3

NEVER CHANGING

Trust in the LORD forever,
for the LORD, the LORD himself, is the Rock eternal.

ISAIAH 26:4 NIV

If we put a rock in a box, it will look the exact same years later. Rocks don't change. The same is true about God. He does not change. He is steady, reliable, and he always keeps his promises.

You can trust God. He will not let you down. It isn't possible for him to change his mind, go against his Word, or break a promise. Everything he says in the Bible will be true forever.

God, you are my rock. I trust you with my life.

JULY 4

GOOD SOIL

> "The seed on good soil stands for those with an honest and good heart. Those people hear the message. They keep it in their hearts. They remain faithful and produce a good crop."
>
> LUKE 8:15 NIRV

Sometimes we hear things from God without really listening. This is like a seed that is planted on a rock. It won't grow because there is nothing for it to dig its roots into. It needs healthy soil to produce good fruit.

If you want God's Word to grow in your heart, it needs good soil. This means that you take what you read, think about it, and do it.

Lord, thank you for your Word. Help me have good soil in my heart so I can listen to what you say.

JULY 5

TOO GOOD FOR WORDS

Lord our God, you have done many miracles.
Your plans for us are many.
If I tried to tell them all,
there would be too many to count.

PSALM 40:5 ICB

We cannot count all the good things God has done. The list would be never-ending. We could spend all our days trying to think through them, and we wouldn't have enough time. He has done so many wonderful things!

What good things has God done in your life so far? What has he done in the lives of your family or friends? How have you seen him move in other parts of the world? Evidence of his love and goodness is everywhere.

God, you are too great for words. Thank you for filling the world with your goodness.

BUILD MUSCLES

Training the body has some value. But being godly has value in every way. It promises help for the life you are now living and the life to come.

1 TIMOTHY 4:8 NIRV

It's good to have a healthy body, but spiritual health is important too. We can exercise in godliness and become stronger. We can build spiritual muscles just like we can build the muscles in our body.

When you practice walking in godliness, it will benefit every area of your life. You can read the Bible, talk to God in prayer, worship him, and look for opportunities to do what he says.

> God, help me honor you with my actions and build my spiritual muscles.

JULY 7

DON'T WORRY

"Don't worry. Don't say, 'What will we eat?' Or, 'What will we drink?' Or, 'What will we wear?' Your Father who is in heaven knows that you need them."

MATTHEW 6:31-32 NIRV

God is aware of our needs. Not only does he know what we need, he promises to provide it for us. He says that if we focus on him, he will take care of everything.

When you belong to God, you can truly rest. You don't have to chase after the same things the world does. You don't have to worry about having what you need. Put God first and remember that he is capable of handling everything.

God, help me not to worry about things I can't control.

JULY 8

GENTLE WORDS

> A gentle answer turns anger away.
> But mean words stir up anger.
>
> PROVERBS 15:1 NIRV

In the middle of an argument, it can be hard to watch our tongues. Without self-control we will probably say something we shouldn't. It's important to choose our words carefully and do our best to be gentle.

Gentle words help everybody calm down. They will keep your heart soft, and they can help end an argument. Most of the time, people don't want to fight with someone who is quiet and calm. Today, practice being gentle with your words.

God, please help me to use gentle and kind words.

JULY 9

STEP BY STEP

"Whoever can be trusted with a little can also be trusted with a lot."

LUKE 16:10 NCV

Step-by-step is always the best way to go. Whether we are building a treehouse, solving a math problem, or cooking a meal, each step matters. We can't skip ahead to something we aren't ready for.

God knows exactly what you can do. He leads you through life one step at a time. He won't skip steps, and he won't give you responsibilities you aren't able to manage. He will strengthen you bit by bit, always preparing you for what's ahead of you.

God, thank you for building me up perfectly.
I trust you to carry me through life.

JULY 10

YOUR ANCHOR

We have this hope as an anchor for the soul, firm and secure.

HEBREWS 6:19 NIV

When a ship drops its anchor, it sits on the bottom of the sea. It keeps the ship in one area, so it doesn't drift off. It keeps the ship secure when waves and wind want to move it around. Even though the ship is big and strong, it still needs an anchor.

You are like a ship. Even if you are big and strong, you still need an anchor. Your hope in Jesus is the strong anchor in your life. It will keep you steady in any storm.

God, thank you for my anchor of hope.
Keep me steady as I trust in Jesus.

JULY 11

EVERY MORNING

> The LORD loves us very much.
> His great love is new every morning.
>
> LAMENTATIONS 3:22-23 NIRV

Every day is a fresh new start. Even if yesterday was hard, today is new. We can give God our worries and start over again. When we put our troubles into his hands, he takes care of them.

God loves you so much! He doesn't want you to carry yesterday's worries into today. Talk to him about your troubles and let him handle them. Enjoy the new morning and look toward the day with hope.

God, thank you for a new start every morning.

JULY 12

PROVE IT

> Here is how God has shown his love for us. While we were still sinners, Christ died for us.
>
> ROMANS 5:8 NIRV

God doesn't just say that he loves us. He shows that he loves us with his actions. Because he sent Jesus to die for our sins, we can know God's love is real. God has proven that his words have meaning.

If you say something but don't act it out, your words don't mean very much. It's important for your actions to line up with what you say. All of God's actions line up with his Word.

God, thank you for sending Jesus so I can know how much you love me.

JULY 13

GOD KNOWS

> LORD, test me. Try me out.
> Look deep down into my heart and mind.
>
> PSALM 26:2 NIRV

Even when we can't make sense of our feelings, God knows our hearts. Even when we don't know what to say, God knows our thoughts. Even when we are unsure, God knows exactly what to do.

God always knows the full story. He knows what you think and what you feel. He can help you understand your feelings and teach you how to make good choices.

God, look into my heart. Help me honor you with my thoughts and actions.

JULY 14

BEAUTIFUL CREATION

> Ever since the world was created it has been possible to see the qualities of God that are not seen.
>
> ROMANS 1:20 NIRV

Nature teaches us about God. Look at all the amazing things he created: a big sky full of stars, a deep ocean full of intricate creatures, and tall mountains that stretch up to the clouds.

The earth is full of amazing things. Each wonderful part of creation tells a story about who God is. You can look at everything he's done and worship him for being so good. Every time you enjoy his creation, thank him.

God, thank you for this beautiful world you created for me to enjoy.

JULY 15

WITHOUT WORRY

"You cannot add any time to your life by worrying about it."
MATTHEW 6:27 ICB

Worrying doesn't get us anywhere. It doesn't solve problems, make us feel better, prepare us for the future, or add time to our lives. Worry is a heavy burden that we don't need to carry.

You can give your worries to God. He is happy to take them from you. In exchange, he will give you peace. He will remind you that he is in control. He loves you, and he wants you to be free from worry.

God, fill my heart with peace. Take my worries and teach me how to trust you with my life.

JULY 16

LET GO OF HATE

> Hatred stirs up conflict,
> but love covers over all wrongs.
>
> PROVERBS 10:12 NIV

When we hold onto hatred, we cannot see each other the right way. Everything becomes a problem, and we are constantly annoyed. This is because hatred stirs up conflict. When we keep something hidden in our heart, it will spill out into our actions.

When you are hurt, the best thing to do is to talk to the person who hurt you and discuss what happened. Explain why you are hurt. You can't always control how other people act, but you can control what you keep in your heart.

God, give me the courage to solve my problems with kind words and forgiveness.

JULY 17

YOUR LIGHT

"You are the light of the world—like a city on a hilltop that cannot be hidden."

Matthew 5:14 NLT

One candle can light up a whole room. It's only one flame, but the light is bright in the darkness. When we know Jesus, we are like that light. When we love others and speak kindly, we can bring hope and encouragement to dark places.

Hiding your light is like having a wonderful gift for a friend but keeping it under your bed. When you have something good, the best thing to do is share it. When you know the truth about God's love, it is good to share it.

God, thank you for giving me a light to share.

JULY 18

DON'T HIDE

> If we confess our sins, he is faithful and righteous to forgive us our sins and to cleanse us from all unrighteousness.
>
> 1 JOHN 1:9 NLT

Secrets can be heavy and hard to carry. In the moment, it might feel good to get away with something, but eventually our secrets will come out. It is better to be honest than to try and cover up our mistakes.

God doesn't want you to hide your flaws. He wants you to be free and full of peace and joy. He promises that when you confess your sins and talk about your mistakes, he will forgive you.

God, thank you for promising to always forgive my sins.

JULY 19

LOVE YOUR ENEMIES

"Love your enemies, do good to them."

Luke 6:35 NIV

As followers of Jesus, we are supposed to love everyone. It is easy to love people who love us, but the Bible says to love even those who do wrong to us. With God's help, we can love people who are hard to love.

Is there someone in your life who is difficult to be around? You can pray for them and be kind even when they don't deserve it. After all, God loves you even when you don't deserve it!

> God, help me to love people even when I think they don't deserve it.

JULY 20

LOVE EQUALLY

> You are making some people more important than others, and with evil thoughts you are deciding that one person is better.
>
> JAMES 2:4 NCV

It is easy to judge others based on what we see, but this is not how God has asked us to treat people. He sees past the outside and looks deep into our hearts. He asks us to try to do the same.

Do your best to treat everybody with the same amount of love and respect. If someone dresses differently or acts differently than you, that doesn't mean they are less important. If you think you are treating others unfairly, ask God for forgiveness. He will help you love like he does.

God, thank you for seeing us all equally. Help me to love people the same way you do.

JULY 21

PERFECT TIMING

> There is a time for everything,
> and a season for every activity under the heavens.
> He has made everything beautiful in its time.
>
> ECCLESIASTES 3:1 NIV

Sometimes we pray and it seems like nothing happens. Instead of being discouraged or thinking God isn't listening, it helps to remember that he knows better than we do. He sees everything perfectly.

It is important to trust God's answers even when they aren't what you want. Sometimes he says yes. Sometimes he says no, and sometimes he says to wait. God knows best, and his timing is perfect.

God, thank you for your perfect timing. Help me to trust in you even when I don't get what I want.

JULY 22

FEAR OF MAN

> Fear of man will prove to be a snare,
> but whoever trusts in the Lord is kept safe.
>
> PROVERBS 29:25 NIV

Fear of man is when we are concerned with what other people think. If we are more worried about making people happy than we are about pleasing God, we probably have a fear of man. The Bible teaches us that this kind of fear is like a trap.

When you fear man, you might worry about fitting in, wearing the right clothes, or saying the right things. Those thoughts can fill your mind with worry. Instead, put your trust in God; he made you perfect just the way you are.

God, thank you for loving me well. Help me to be more concerned with what you think than with what other people think.

JULY 23

WHAT GOD WANTS

> We are confident that he hears whenever we ask for anything that pleases him.
>
> 1 JOHN 5:14 NLT

When we know someone well, we know what they like and dislike. We know our parents want us to eat well, so if we ask for some vegetables, they will probably say yes. We also know that if we ask for cookies before dinner, they will probably say no.

In the same way, the more you get to know God, the more confidence you'll have when you pray. When you know what he likes and dislikes, you won't be surprised or confused by what he says to you.

God, thank you that I can ask you for whatever I need.

JULY 24

WAIT PATIENTLY

God's people need to be very patient. They are the ones who obey God's commands. And they remain faithful to Jesus.

REVELATION 14:12 NIRV

As God's people, we have to patient. This is because one day, Jesus will come back again. He will make all things right and will wipe every tear from our eyes. We have to wait patiently for that day.

Waiting on God's promises isn't always easy. On days when it's hard, remember that God can give you strength. He can help you live the right way and stay faithful to Jesus. When you are impatient, remember that good things are coming.

God, help me to grow in patience. I want to listen to your commands while I wait for Jesus.

LEADERSHIP

> Choose some capable men from among the people.
> Choose men who respect God and who can be trusted.
>
> EXODUS 18:21 ICB

The Bible is full of descriptions of good and bad leaders. Being in front of other people, teaching them and guiding them, is something God takes seriously. He calls leaders to be honest, upright, and capable. They should respect God and not be tempted by power or money.

If you want to be a leader, it's important to follow God's instructions. You must put the needs of others before your own and be willing to do hard things.

God, thank you for the good leaders in my life. Help me to grow into someone who can be a good leader.

JULY 26

EXAMPLE TO FOLLOW

> Follow my example, as I follow the example of Christ.
>
> 1 CORINTHIANS 11:1 ICB

We often follow others. We look to people who are older and wiser to show us the way. We see the way they live, and we do our best to do the same. It's important to make sure we are following people who follow Jesus.

If you ask him to, God will put people in your life whom you can follow. Listen closely as they teach you about Jesus. Ask questions and do your best to learn from them.

*God, I want to learn more about you.
Please put people in my life who can teach me.*

JULY 27

NO ONE ELSE

> From long ago no one has ever heard of a God like you.
> No one has ever seen a God besides you,
> who helps the people who trust you.
>
> ISAIAH 64:4 NCV

The God we serve is the one true God! There has never been another like him, and there never will be. He alone is truly compassionate, kind, holy, and mighty. No one else compares to him.

Throughout your life, you might hear many people claim to know who God is. If the God they describe doesn't match up with the Bible, their story is false. Your heavenly Father is full of love and mercy, and no one can take his place.

God, give me confidence in who you are! Keep me from being swayed by the stories of others.

JULY 28

HE KNOWS

God supplies seed for the person who plants. He supplies bread for food. God will also supply and increase the amount of your seed. He will increase the results of your good works.

2 CORINTHIANS 9:10 NIRV

God sees each of us. He knows what we need, and he is happy to help us. He takes care of each person according to what they need, even if it is different from another person. He sees each situation perfectly.

God sees everything you do. He says he will give you what you need and will make sure you are taken care of. He helps you because he wants to, and because it's ingrained in his very character to take care of you.

God, I'm so glad you know exactly what I need! I trust you to take care of me.

JULY 29

HUMBLE

Always be humble and gentle. Be patient with each other, making allowance for each other's faults because of your love.

EPHESIANS 4:2 NCV

No one is perfect. We all make mistakes, and God asks us to be kind to each other even when someone does the wrong thing. We are supposed to treat each other with understanding and realize we all mess up from time to time.

It is always best to be humble. Being humble means realizing you make just as many mistakes as the person next to you. When someone around you does something wrong, remember how you want to be treated when you make a mistake.

God, forgive me for the times I've made people feel bad for their mistakes. Teach me to be patient and kind.

JULY 30

MORE THAN WORDS

> "These people show honor to me with words, but their hearts are far from me."
>
> MARK 7:6 NCV

When our words don't line up with our actions, something is out of order. What we do should match up with what we say. If it doesn't, we should take a look at what is going on in our hearts.

Talking about God is great, but it's more important that he has your heart. If your relationship with God is only about words, then it isn't very deep. Spend time with him, get to know him, and let him love you.

God, take my whole heart. Keep me close to you and teach me your ways. I love you.

JULY 31

NO MORE DARKNESS

> He brought them out of their gloom and darkness.
> He broke their chains.
>
> PSALM 107:14 ICB

Looking for something in the dark is difficult. We might bump into things, stub our toes, or get frustrated. It's really hard to see without any light. Light makes all the difference when something is lost.

Living your life without Jesus is like searching for something in the dark. Jesus is light, and he will show you the way. It doesn't make sense to wander around in the dark when you don't have to. As a follower of Jesus, you get to walk in the light.

God, thank you for saving me from darkness and showing me the right way to live.

AUGUST

Lord, you will give perfect peace
to those who commit themselves
to be faithful to you.
That's because they trust in you.

Isaiah 26:3 nirv

AUGUST 1

FAITHFULNESS

"I have brought you glory on earth by finishing the work you gave me to do."

JOHN 17:4 NIV

It feels good to finish a task or project. When we do something all the way, we are faithful. It is not faithful to do a job halfway. Faithfulness is all about sticking to what we said we were going to do.

Jesus was completely faithful. Going to the cross was not an easy thing for him to finish, but he knew that it was God's plan. Because of his faithfulness, you can have eternal life.

God, help me to be faithful with what I am given to do.

AUGUST 2

STAY CALM

> "You will receive the strength you need when you stay calm and trust in me."
>
> ISAIAH 30:15 NIRV

We can't control the problems we might face, but we can control how we respond to them. We don't know what types of storms we will walk through, but we know for sure that God is strong enough to handle it.

When something difficult happens, stay calm. Take deep breaths, let God fill you with peace, and remember he is in control. He promises to strengthen you when you trust in him.

God, help me trust in you. Thank you for the strength you give me when I look to you.

AUGUST 3

IT IS TRUE

> The word of the Lord holds true,
> and we can trust everything he does.
>
> PSALM 33:4 NLT

When our word holds true, it means that what we say is proven to be right. It means we are reliable and can be trusted. God's Word holds true. Everything he says is good and right.

This means you can depend on him! If he says he will take care of you, you don't have to worry. If he says he will lead you through life, you don't have to wonder what to do. If he says he loves you, you know it is true.

God, help me to trust your Word. Fill my heart with truth and remind me of your goodness.

AUGUST 4

NEW LIFE

> Anyone who belongs to Christ has become a new person.
> The old life is gone; a new life has begun!
>
> 2 CORINTHIANS 5:17 NLT

When we choose to follow Jesus, something miraculous happens! We are changed into a completely new person. We are set free from our sins, and we are made perfect because of Christ.

Jesus has given you a fresh start. No matter what mistakes you've made, you are forgiven when you ask him to forgive you. He takes your sins, and he gets rid of them. It's as if they never existed.

Jesus, thank you for making me new.

AUGUST 5

LOVING WORDS

> We use our tongues to praise our Lord and Father, but then we curse people, whom God made like himself.
>
> JAMES 3:9 NCV

Our words and our hearts should say the same thing. It isn't right to say we love God but use our words to be unkind to others. Each person is made in God's image and is worthy of being loved and made to feel important.

It's important to God that you don't use your words to hurt people. If you've ever been put down, laughed at, or made to feel small, you also know how powerful words are. Use your words to praise God and love others.

God, fill me with your love and help me to be kind with what I say.

AUGUST 6

SLOW TO ANGER

> You are a God who forgives.
> You are gracious.
> You are tender and kind.
> You are slow to get angry.
> You are full of love.
>
> NEHEMIAH 9:17 NIRV

God is kind and slow to get angry. He isn't fazed by the things that cause anger to stir within us. He is patient and understanding. He sees our hearts, and he looks at us with tenderness.

When you make mistakes, God is not angry. When you do something wrong, he is not outraged. He is not looking down at you with frustration. He is not disappointed in you or annoyed with your failures. He sees you with mercy and love.

God, show me what you are really like.
Fill me with your love and grace.

AUGUST 7

GOOD CHOICES

> When you are tempted, God will give you a way out. Then you will be able to deal with it.
>
> 1 CORINTHIANS 10:13 NIRV

When you are tempted, it can be hard to make the right choice. Sometimes doing the wrong thing seems like such a good idea! When this happens, it's important to remember that God is ready to help.

When you are tempted, God promises to give you a way out. He will give you strength and help you say no when you need to. The more you ask him for help, the better you will get at doing the right thing.

God, thank you for helping me make good choices.

AUGUST 8

CONSTANT HELPER

> Don't you know that you are God's temple and that God's Spirit lives in you?
>
> 1 CORINTHIANS 3:16 NCV

When Jesus went back to heaven, he left us with the wonderful gift of his Spirit, so we would never be alone. When we choose to follow Jesus, his Spirit lives within us. He guides us through life, and he helps us stay close to God.

Don't forget that you have a helper at all times! He is in you, helping you with every part of your day. He will remind you of truth and help you make wise choices.

Jesus, thank you for the gift of the Holy Spirit. Thank you for giving me a helper who keeps me steady.

AUGUST 9

GREATEST TREASURE

"I will give you the wealth that is stored away.
And I will give you hidden riches."

ISAIAH 45:3 ICB

God's love is the greatest treasure of all. His blessings are like shiny coins or precious gems. He has given wonderful gifts to each of his children. If we pay attention, we will see the great riches we have because of him.

Every good thing in your life comes from God. He gives you blessings now, but the greatest treasure is waiting for you in eternity.

God, help me to remember that your love is my greatest treasure.

AUGUST 10

LOVE OTHERS

> "Do for other people the same things
> you want them to do for you."
> MATTHEW 7:12 ICB

We all want to be loved and taken care of. We all want to be included and thought of. It's important that we treat everyone around us in the same way we want to be treated. We honor God when we are kind, thoughtful, and loving toward others.

You can't control how other people behave. If you treat others well, they might not return the favor. Even if this happens, God sees your love for others, and he is pleased.

God, help me to love others well no matter how I am treated. Teach me how to love like you.

AUGUST 11

GOD HELPS

> My help comes from the Lord.
> He made heaven and earth.
>
> PSALM 121:2 ICB

God created the sky and the earth with just a few words. If he did that, he can help us with any problem we face. There is nothing in our lives that is too big for him to handle. He has everything we need.

When you have a problem, do you turn to God? You're not alone if you look for help in other places. It takes practice to run to God quickly when something goes wrong. When you have a problem, remember God wants to help you!

God, you are so strong and can help me with anything!

AUGUST 12

GOD'S SONG

*The Lord your God is with you.
He will sing and be joyful about you.*

ZEPHANIAH 3:17 ICB

God is not far away. The Bible says that he is singing over us. He sings a happy song because he cares for us so much. He wants us to know that we are safe and loved.

You are so important to God! He cares for you more than anyone else can. He carefully created you, and he is so proud that you are his son. He wants you to know that you make him happy.

Dear God, help me to remember how much you love me.

AUGUST 13

PRAY ALL THE TIME

> Never stop praying.
> 1 THESSALONIANS 5:17 ICB

Talking is really important in any relationship. It's how we communicate and learn about each other. Without talking, it would be much harder to share our thoughts and feelings.

When you pray, you are talking with God. You can talk to him about anything. You can tell him your worries, thank him for the good things in your life, and ask him for what you need. God loves it when you talk to him!

God, thank you for listening when I talk to you.

AUGUST 14

ALL FOR GOD

In all the work you are doing, work the best you can.

COLOSSIANS 3:23 ICB

Each day is filled with many activities. We get dressed, make our bed, and brush our teeth. We learn, play with friends, and spend time with our family. No matter what we are doing, we should do our best.

Every single task you do can be approached with a good attitude and a sense of excellence. If you are making your bed, do it the best you can. If you are playing with friends, strive to be as kind as possible. No matter what is in front of you, work at it with all your heart.

God, help me to do my best in all I do.

AUGUST 15

SAY NO TO PRIDE

> Pride leads only to shame.
> It is wise not to be proud.
>
> PROVERBS 11:2 ICB

There is a difference between being proud of something we've done and acting with pride. It's okay to recognize hard work, but it's not okay to think that we are better than anyone else.

If you are prideful, you probably don't like admitting when you are wrong. You might be afraid to make mistakes or worry that people will look down on you. The Bible says that pride only leads to shame. Instead of being prideful, remember that everyone makes mistakes and it's okay to admit it.

God, please help me to learn from my mistakes. Teach me how to be humble instead of prideful.

AUGUST 16

SWEET WORDS

> How sweet your words taste to me;
> they are sweeter than honey.
>
> PSALM 119:103 NLT

God's Word is sweet and refreshing. It is like a big glass of water on a hot, summer day. It's like a delicious meal when we are really hungry. The Bible is ours to explore and learn from. It's a wonderful gift from God!

Get into the habit of reading God's Word every chance you get. Be encouraged by what he has to say. When you feel lost, look to the examples of others in the Bible.

God, thank you for your Word! Help me understand what it means for my life.

AUGUST 17

NO FEAR

> The Lord is my light and my salvation—
> so why should I be afraid?
> The Lord is my fortress,
> protecting me from danger,
> so why should I tremble?
>
> PSALM 27:1 NLT

It is okay to feel afraid. It is normal to be nervous sometimes. Everyone is afraid at different times, but God doesn't want us to stay in that fear. He doesn't want us to feel that way all the time, and he doesn't want us to let fear be in control.

When you feel fear creeping up, talk to God. Tell him about your fears and ask him for help. He loves to give you strength when you ask for it. He is bigger than your greatest fear.

God, thank you for being big enough to handle my fears.

AUGUST 18

USE THE INSTRUCTIONS

All Scripture is God-breathed and is useful for teaching, rebuking, correcting and training in righteousness.

2 TIMOTHY 3:16 NIV

Putting together a Lego kit without instructions is difficult. Some steps might be missed, or we might do something incorrectly. It would be a lot easier and more fun to just use the instructions. If we have them, it doesn't make sense not to use them.

This is how you can think about the Bible. All of it is good and helpful for living. The Bible can teach you what is right and wrong. It can encourage you and bring you joy. It would be silly not to use something so good and helpful!

God, thank you for your Word.
Teach me how to use it well.

AUGUST 19

WORRY HOLDER

> Turn your worries over to the Lord.
> He will keep you going.
>
> PSALM 55:22 NIRV

Carrying worries around is like hiking with a backpack full of rocks. The extra weight makes everything harder. It doesn't make sense to carry around something that cannot be useful.

Take your worries and hand them to God. You'll find that your load will get lighter, and it will be easier to move forward. There is no limit to what God can carry. He is stronger than you are, and he can keep you going in the right direction.

God, thank you for being strong enough to carry my worries.

AUGUST 20

HOW TO LOVE

"Love your neighbor as you love yourself." If you obey this law, you are doing right. But if you treat one person as being more important than another, you are sinning.

JAMES 2:8-9 NCV

There are certain things that are clear and obvious in the Bible. Loving others is one of those things. We are told to love others as much as we love ourselves. This means that we are supposed to treat each person we meet with the same kindness and respect that we want to be treated with.

Today, focus on treating others how you want to be treated. Your words should lift others up and make them feel loved. Your actions should be gentle and make other people feel cared for. Loving the people around you is the most important part of your day.

God, thank you for teaching me how to love others. Show me how I can be kind today.

AUGUST 21

NEVER LOST

> You always show me the path of life.
> You will fill me with joy when I am with you.
> You will make me happy forever at your right hand.
>
> PSALM 16:11 NIRV

If we close our eyes and try to walk around our home, we'll probably bump into a thing or two. It's hard to stay on a path we cannot see. However, if we close our eyes and ask a friend to guide us, we'll end up in the right spot.

When you are following God, you don't have to worry about stumbling around. He promises to always show you the right path. The more time you spend with him, the more familiar you will be with his voice.

God, thank you for leading me. Help me to become more familiar with your voice.

AUGUST 22

SPEAK UP

> Speak up for those who cannot speak for themselves;
> defend the rights of all those who have nothing.
> Speak up and judge fairly, and defend the rights of the poor
> and needy.
>
> PROVERBS 31:8-9 NCV

Jesus always spoke up for those who could not defend themselves. As his followers, we should do the same. He wants us to be kind when everyone else is leaving someone out.

When someone is being treated unfairly, you can speak up and defend them. You have a voice, and you can help. There are always opportunities to be kind. Today, ask God to show you who needs some extra love.

God, show me opportunities to speak up for those who cannot speak for themselves.

AUGUST 23

THE GREATEST DAD

> See how very much our Father loves us, for he calls us his children, and that is what we are!
>
> 1 JOHN 3:1 NLT

God is not just a mighty ruler. He is not just a powerful king. He is also a loving father. God loves us so much that he calls us his children! We have the biggest, strongest, and best Dad in the whole wide world.

When you see yourself as a son of God, you will be confident in who you are. As a son, you have unlimited access to God. He has made you part of his family, and he wants you to feel safe and secure in his love.

God, thank you for being a kind and loving father. Help me to understand that I am your son.

AUGUST 24

ALL YOU WANT

> I'm asking the Lord for only one thing.
> Here is what I want.
> I want to live in the house of the Lord
> all the days of my life.
>
> PSALM 27:4 NIRV

When we really want something, it's all we can think about. Whether we are longing for summer vacation, Christmas morning, or a visit from someone we love, we are filled with excitement and anticipation.

This is how you are meant to see God. The more time you spend with him, the more you will love being near him. Thoughts of him will fill your mind, and you will be excited to worship him.

God, I want you to be at the top of my priority list.
Fill me with love for you.

THOUGHTFUL

We should help others do what is right and build them up in the Lord. For even Christ didn't live to please himself.

ROMANS 15:1-3 NLT

Sometimes the right thing is simply what is best for someone else. This is how Jesus lived and how we should live as well. If we all think about how to help each other, we will all be well taken care of.

Your needs and wants are important, but so are the needs and wants of the people around you. The Bible says to do what is best for others and not just yourself. This isn't always easy to do, but it is God's way of doing things.

> God, help me to think about others before myself. Teach me how to be selfless and kind.

AUGUST 26

HONESTY

> Kings are pleased when what you say is honest.
> They value people who speak what is right.
>
> PROVERBS 16:13 NIRV

It is always best to be honest. The Bible says that we will be rewarded for our honesty. Whether we see those rewards now or when Jesus comes back, God promises good things will come from telling the truth.

Truth brings freedom, while hiding your mistakes only creates shame. When you do something wrong, don't try to cover it up. Be truthful about what you've done and ask God to help you. He will teach you how to move forward.

God, help me to always be honest. Give me strength to tell the truth even when it's difficult.

AUGUST 27

YOU BELONG

"Do not be afraid. I will set you free.
I will send for you by name. You belong to me."

ISAIAH 43:1 NIRV

There might be times in life when we feel lost in the crowd. Maybe we wish we got more attention from our parents, or we don't have a lot of close friends. No matter the situation, it's normal to sometimes feel overlooked.

You are important to God. You are significant to him. It doesn't matter how many people there are on this earth, he sees you. He is a good father who notices and cares for each of his children. You belong to the Creator of the entire universe.

God, thank you for seeing me! Help me to remember that I belong to you.

AUGUST 28

HIGHLY ESTEEMED

> A good name is more desirable than great riches;
> to be esteemed is better than silver or gold.
>
> PROVERBS 22:1 NIV

When someone is esteemed, it means other people think highly of them. When someone has a good name, it means they are well liked because of their character or reputation. A good name must be earned. It is based on the way we act and how we treat people.

Your name is more important than what you have. In other words, your riches are meaningless if your actions cause people to think poorly of you. Being honest, kind, reliable, and hard working is more valuable than having money or things.

God, I want my character to honor you!
Help me make a good name for myself.

AUGUST 29

DRIFT

> Don't let me drift toward evil
> or take part in acts of wickedness.
> Don't let me share in the delicacies
> of those who do wrong.
>
> PSALM 141:4 NLT

We all make mistakes, but it's important to admit when we are wrong and adjust our course. If we continue to do the wrong thing, we will quickly find ourselves on a path we don't want. A lot of small decisions can lead to big consequences.

Often, the small decisions you make each day decide the direction of your life. This is why God reminds you to be on guard. He graciously shows you how to honor him every day. Each good decision adds up to a lifetime of being faithful.

God, help me to follow you all my days. Keep me from making bad decisions.

AUGUST 30

THE SAME GOD

> God is not a man,
> so he does not lie.
> He is not human,
> so he does not change his mind.
>
> NUMBERS 23:19 NLT

We can trust the Word of God. He keeps his promises, and he always tells the truth. He doesn't change his mind. He is always the same. Everything he says is reliable and perfect.

If God says he loves you, then it is true for eternity. If he says he cares for you, then he always will. He is the same God to you as he was to the people who lived in the Bible. The same God who led the Israelites through the Red Sea will lead you through whatever you are facing.

God, when I feel far from you, remind me you are near.

AUGUST 31

UNSHAKEABLE

> Let us be thankful, because we have a kingdom that cannot be shaken. We should worship God in a way that pleases him with respect and fear.
>
> HEBREWS 12:28 NCV

Life is full of changes. We move to new towns, gain and lose friends, and we change as we grow up. There aren't many things that stay exactly the same. Even the earth shifts and evolves. When everything around us is moving or shaking, we can rely on God.

As a follower of Jesus, you are part of a kingdom that cannot be shaken. You stand on a firm foundation that will never crumble. Anytime you feel unsteady, you can lean on Jesus.

God, teach me how to depend on you when everything around me is changing.

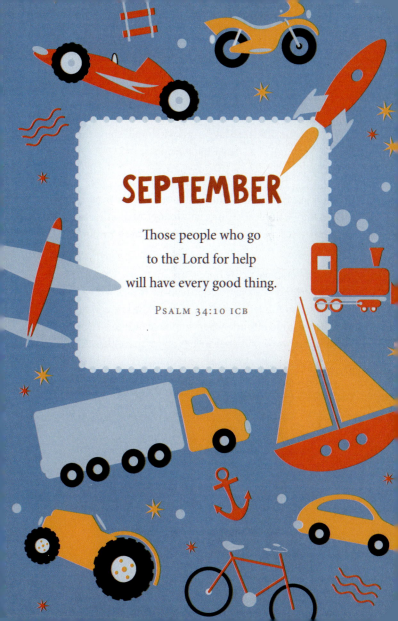

SEPTEMBER

Those people who go to the Lord for help will have every good thing.

PSALM 34:10 ICB

SEPTEMBER 1

REAL LOVE

Our love must be true love. And we should show that love by what we do.

1 JOHN 3:18 ICB

It's easy to say we love someone, but it's harder to turn those words into actions. It's important to love each other with more than just our words. The Bible says to show our love by what we do.

Each day you have many opportunities to use your actions to love others. You can share your favorite things with a brother or sister. You can let someone else have the last cookie. You can have a good attitude when someone else gets their way. All of these show that your love is about more than words.

God, show me how I can love with my actions.

SEPTEMBER 2

SEEK AND FIND

> "I love those who love me,
> and those who seek me find me."
>
> PROVERBS 8:17 NIV

God wants to be found. He wants us to look for him because we love him. He is never hiding from us, and he is always ready to respond to our cries.

You get to be as close to God as you want to be. There is nothing holding you back from being in his presence. He loves it when you are near to him and when you look for him with all your heart. Run to God, and he will always welcome you fully.

*God, fill my heart with love for you.
I want more of you in my life.*

SEPTEMBER 3

THROUGH WILDERNESS

> "Then I will lead the blind along a way they never knew.
> I will guide them along paths they have not known.
> I will make the darkness become light for them."
>
> ISAIAH 42:16 ICB

God leads us perfectly. He makes sure we don't get into trouble, and he shows us which way to go. He can see things we cannot see. If we trust his leadership, we will stay on the right path.

If you've ever followed a guide through the wilderness, you've seen a little glimpse of what God's leadership is like. He can help you with the parts of life that are new. He knows what each of your days will look like, and he is the perfect guide.

*God, thank you for being a perfect leader.
Help me to trust what you say.*

SEPTEMBER 4

SERVE OTHERS

"The greatest among you must be a servant."
MATTHEW 23:11

There is nothing greater than serving others. While some jobs may seem important, serving others has more value than anything else. Jesus served us by laying down his life for our salvation. We can serve others by putting their needs first.

It doesn't matter if other people notice your good acts. Part of serving others is doing it for God and not yourself. Practice doing kind things without anyone praising you for it.

God, show me opportunities to serve others.

SEPTEMBER 5

KIND LIKE GOD

A kind person is doing himself a favor.
But a cruel person brings trouble on himself.

PROVERBS 11:17 ICB

Kindness is attractive. When we are kind, other people want to be around us. When we go out of our way to make people feel noticed and important, we show them what God is like. God is always kind.

Every day you have opportunities to be kind. You can stand up for someone who is being left out. You can help your parents without complaining. You can cheer up your brother or sister when they are sad. Kindness notices others and puts them first.

God, you have been so kind to me! I want my actions to make other people feel loved and important.

SEPTEMBER 6

WEIGHT OF WORRY

Worry makes a person feel as if he is carrying a heavy load.
But a kind word cheers up a person.

PROVERBS 12:25 ICB

We often find ourselves thinking too much about the wrong things. We start to worry about how we look, what other people think, or if we'll get what we want. These kinds of worries feel heavy in our minds, and they are hard to carry.

Isn't it great when your parents or friends tell you everything is going to be alright? They might make you laugh or encourage you when you are fearful. Kind words are good for everyone, and they need to be shared!

> God, help me to be an encouraging friend
> who brings peace to those around me.

SEPTEMBER 7

POWERFUL

"I will go before you.
And I will make the mountains flat.
I will break down the bronze gates of the cities.
I will cut through the iron bars on the gates."

ISAIAH 45:2 ICB

If we think of the most powerful thing that exists, we might imagine a huge mountain, crashing waves, or a roaring lion. Few things can stand in the way of something that powerful.

God is more powerful than anything you can think of. He is stronger than you can imagine, and he loves to use his strength to rescue his people. What a mighty God you have on your side!

God, thank you for your great strength.
I am in awe of how powerful you are.

SEPTEMBER 8

IN THE MORNING

> Every morning he wakes me.
> He teaches me to listen like a student.
>
> ISAIAH 50:4 NCV

Most people have a morning routine. Some of us wake up and stay snuggled in our beds for a while. Some of us open our eyes and are ready to eat breakfast right away. No matter what our habits are, it's important to start the day in a healthy way.

There are healthy habits that are good for your body, and there are healthy habits that are good for your soul. Taking time to be with God in the morning is good for your heart. When you start the day with God, you are starting your day the best way possible.

God, help me to spend time with you today.

SEPTEMBER 9

WONDERFULLY MADE

> Thank you for making me so wonderfully complex!
> Your workmanship is marvelous—how well I know it.
>
> PSALM 139:14 NLT

God is wildly creative. He has knit together billions of people, and none of us are exactly alike. We are each wonderfully complex. We look, act, feel, and think differently. We are each completely unique, yet somehow, we are all made in God's image.

Every beautiful thing you notice about yourself is a glimpse of who God is. You reflect the one true God. He made you with care, and he wants you to know how precious you are to him.

God, I am thankful for the way you made me. Help me see the ways I reflect who you are.

SEPTEMBER 10

BIG SMILE

> He has glory and majesty; he has power and joy in his Temple.
>
> 1 CHRONICLES 16:27 NCV

We often think about how God is strong, powerful, mighty, and glorious. It's important to remember that God is also really happy. He is full of joy! Imagine God with a huge smile on his face.

Have you ever thought about God as happy? He is not angry or rude. He is not mean or harsh. God, your heavenly Father, is kind and joyful. He has glory and majesty, and he is delighted by you.

God, forgive me for the times I have thought of you as angry. Help me see you as you really are.

SEPTEMBER 11

GENTLE WORDS

*With patience you can convince a ruler,
and a gentle word can get through to the hard-headed.*

PROVERBS 25:15 NCV

We've all gotten into arguments that go around and around. Neither person wants to admit they are wrong, and the same words are said over and over. Instead of being frustrated or stubborn, patience and gentleness are always better.

When you want to share what you think, yelling or arguing does not help. It only makes the problem bigger. Gentle words are best. Your most powerful weapon is a soft and gentle word.

God, help me to speak in a way that shows love.
Teach me how to speak gently and kindly.

SEPTEMBER 12

LOVE ENDURES

> Love patiently accepts all things. It always trusts, always hopes, and always endures.
>
> 1 CORINTHIANS 13:7 NCV

Endurance means being unwilling to quit. Endurance is finishing what we've started even when it's hard. Endurance means staying steady until the very end.

The Bible says that love endures. This means it never gives up. Even when you go through something difficult, God's love will never give up on you. His love endures through everything.

God, thank you for your enduring love. Thank you for being with me even when life is hard.

SEPTEMBER 13

THE HOLY SPIRIT

"When the Spirit of truth comes, he will lead you into all truth."

JOHN 16:13 NCV

Whether we've tried a new sport, a new instrument, or opened a book for the very first time, we are familiar with learning something new. It's likely that in order to master those new skills, we had someone leading the way. We've had teachers, coaches, and parents help us when we needed it.

Helping is exactly what the Holy Spirit does! He is the one who teaches you everything you need to know about God. He helps you remember the truth you've learned, and he encourages you along the way.

God, thank you for the Holy Spirit. Thank you for a teacher who can always help me when I need it.

SEPTEMBER 14

STARTING AGAIN

> You were taught to be made new in your hearts,
> to become a new person.
>
> EPHESIANS 4:23 NCV

Everyone makes mistakes. We all do the wrong thing sometimes. When we confess what we've done and accept God's mercy, he makes us brand new.

Have you ever wanted to start over? That's what following Jesus is like. When you ask him for forgiveness, he takes away your sins. He gives you grace and helps you walk in a better direction.

God, help me remember that I can always have a new start with your help.

SEPTEMBER 15

EXERCISE YOUR FAITH

> It was by faith that Noah heard God's warnings about things he could not yet see. He obeyed God and built a large boat to save his family.
>
> HEBREWS 11:7 NCV

God asked Noah to do a crazy thing—to build a big boat when it had never rained before. Noah might not have understood why, but he still listened to God. When it started raining, Noah was glad he had obeyed. It took a lot of faith to listen even when he didn't understand.

God wants you to obey him and trust that he knows best. There might be times in your life when his instructions don't make sense to you. In those moments, it's important to trust him and follow his instructions.

God, help me to listen to you even when I don't understand.

SEPTEMBER 16

LEARN AND GROW

> These troubles come to prove that your faith is pure. This purity of faith is worth more than gold, which can be proved to be pure by fire but will ruin.
>
> 1 PETER 1:7 NCV

It would be nice to have a life without troubles. Since that's not possible, it helps to realize that trials aren't all bad. Even our most painful struggles can teach us something and help us grow.

On a hard day, you might realize you have been impatient or unkind. When you notice these things, God can help you with them.

God, help me to see the problems in my life as opportunities to grow. I want to become more like you.

SEPTEMBER 17

THE GOOD LIST

Let all that I am praise the LORD
may I never forget the good things he does for me.

PSALM 103:2 NLT

When we have a hard day, it can be easy to forget all the good things that have happened. We only think about how we feel in the moment. Even when things don't go our way, it's important to remember that God is still good.

It can be really helpful to keep a list of all the good things God has done for you. Each time you see his goodness, add it to your list. When you're having a rough day, you can look at your list and remember all that God has done.

God, help me to see and remember all that you have done for me.

SEPTEMBER 18

GIFT OF JESUS

> Everyone has sinned; we all fall short of God's glorious standard. Yet God, in his grace, freely makes us right in his sight. He did this through Christ Jesus.
>
> ROMANS 3:23-24 NLT

Sometimes it feels like if we follow all the rules and do all the right things, everything will be okay. But no one can be perfect all the time. We all sin and make mistakes.

What is in your heart is so much more important than what you do. God looks past how good you are, and he sees right inside to the deepest parts of your heart. It is his grace that makes you right, not how well you behave. Put your trust in Jesus and thank him for his grace.

God, thank you that your love doesn't depend on my goodness.

SEPTEMBER 19

ON YOUR TEAM

> Two people are better off than one, for they can help each other succeed. If one person falls, the other can reach out and help. But someone who falls alone is in real trouble.
>
> ECCLESIASTES 4:9-10 NLT

We all need people on our team! God didn't want us to go through life alone. We are supposed to help each other when life is difficult and encourage each other when the days are hard. We are stronger together.

It is always better to have someone by your side. Thank God for the people on your team and think about how you can show them how grateful you are.

God, thank you for the people who love me and help me.

SEPTEMBER 20

EAGER TO SERVE

> When God's people are in need, be ready to help them.
> Always be eager to practice hospitality.
>
> ROMANS 12:13 NLT

As followers of God, we should always be ready to help. We can volunteer our time and energy to serve. Just because you are young doesn't mean you cannot be helpful and welcoming.

You can be generous with whatever you have. You can share your lunch with someone who is hungry, or you can offer to play with someone who is left out. You can help a friend with homework, or you can clean your room without being asked.

God, give me the strength I need to help others.

SEPTEMBER 21

GOD ALWAYS HEARS

Praise the Lord for he has heard my cry for mercy.
I trust him with all my heart.
He helps me, and my heart is filled with joy.

PSALM 28:7 NLT

God is never so far away that he can't hear our cries for help. Isn't that incredible? Whether we calmly ask for help or we cry and scream, God hears us. He wants to be close to us, and he welcomes us when we turn to him.

Don't ever feel like you need to act a certain way for God to hear your prayers. He hears you when you are happy, sad, angry, or impatient. He is always listening, and he loves the sound of your voice.

God, thank you for always listening when I talk to you.

SEPTEMBER 22

HOLDING HANDS

> "I hold you by your right hand—
> I, the LORD your God.
> And I say to you, 'Don't be afraid.
> I am here to help you.'"
>
> ISAIAH 41:13 NLT

In busy crowds, most parents hold their child's hand. With them close by, the little one feels comfortable in new situations. The parents know their way around, and they know how to keep their child safe.

Your relationship with God is the same. He holds you by your hand so he can help you. Not only is he keeping you safe, but he is also letting you know that you aren't alone.

God, thank you for leading me. Thank you for holding my hand and being close to me.

SEPTEMBER 23

GOOD FRUIT

> "Just as you can identify a tree by its fruit, so you can identify people by their actions."
>
> MATTHEW 7:20 NLT

When it's time for the harvest, we collect apples from apple trees and oranges from orange trees. A pear tree won't grow cherries, and an oak tree won't make pinecones. You can tell what type of tree you have by looking at what it creates.

The same is true of people. You can tell a lot about someone by looking at what they do. When someone is following Jesus, they will have the fruit of the Spirit in their life. This means that they will show love, joy, peace, patience, kindness, goodness, faithfulness, gentleness, and self-control.

God, please give me the fruit of the Spirit in my life.

SEPTEMBER 24

TRUE KING

> God made Christ more important than all rulers, authorities, powers, and kings.
>
> EPHESIANS 1:21 ICB

Jesus is the true King, and he is more important than any government. The world is full of different types of leaders, some good and some bad. No matter what the situation is, Jesus deserves our loyalty.

A lot will change in your lifetime. You will see leaders rise and fall. You will see countries at war, and you will see times of peace. No matter what happens or who is in charge, remember that Jesus is your true King.

God, help me remember that Jesus is my true King. Keep from following anyone else.

SEPTEMBER 25

GOOD AND PERFECT

> Whatever is good and perfect is a gift coming down to us from God our Father, who created all the lights in the heavens. He never changes or casts a shifting shadow.
>
> JAMES 1:17 NLT

Life is full of beautiful things! We all have different stories, but we can all experience the goodness of God. If we take a moment and pay attention, we will begin to see the many gifts that God has given us.

God is a good father who loves to give you good gifts. From the beauty of the rising sun to friends and family who love you, every good thing in your life is from him.

God, thank you for filling my days with gifts.

SEPTEMBER 26

INCREDIBLE

> The sky was made at the LORD's command.
> By the breath from his mouth, he made all the stars.
>
> PSALM 33:6 NCV

The world is a miraculous display of God's glory. Each part of the earth shows us how much he cares for us. He could have made any environment for us to live in, but he created stunning sunsets and huge oceans for us to enjoy.

Take some time to look around the world you live in. God's creation is wonderful, and it proves how good he is. Thank him for all he has made and remember how mighty he is.

God, I want to see your goodness in all of creation. Thank you for making such a beautiful world!

SEPTEMBER 27

PRACTICE FORGIVENESS

> Most importantly, love each other deeply, because love will cause people to forgive each other for many sins.
>
> 1 Peter 4:8 NCV

No one is perfect. We all make mistakes. When we love someone well, we keep loving them even when they mess up. Jesus is the perfect example of this.

Jesus continues to love you even when you do the wrong thing over and over again. Just because someone makes a mistake doesn't mean you give up on them or stop loving them. If you want to love others the way Jesus loves you, it's important to practice forgivingness.

God, fill me with your love so I can love others.

SEPTEMBER 28

CONTINUE FOLLOWING

> Continue following the teachings you learned. You know they are true, because you trust those who taught you.
>
> 2 TIMOTHY 3:14 NCV

Following God takes an entire lifetime. Each day we turn our eyes toward him and trust him to lead us. The more we follow him, the more we understand his teachings.

Read the Bible and ask questions. If you find something you don't understand, dig deeper. If you find something you don't like, discuss it with someone you trust. God is not afraid of your questions. He is bigger than any questions you have.

God, thank you for helping me understand your teachings.

SEPTEMBER 29

GET TO KNOW HIM

I pray that your love will grow more and more. And let it be based on knowledge and understanding. Then you will be able to know what is best.

PHILIPPIANS 1:9-10 NIRV

Just like we need to spend time with other people to get to know them, we need to spend time with God. The more we get to know God, the more we will love him. This is what the Bible means when it says our love should be based on knowledge and understanding.

You don't need to love God because someone tells you to. Spend time with him and get to know him. He wants to have a relationship with you.

God, draw me closer to you.
I want to get to know you more!

SEPTEMBER 30

NEVER DISAPPOINTED

> "I will save the one who loves me.
> I will keep him safe, because he trusts in me."
>
> PSALM 91:14 NIRV

God's love is greater than any love we can experience on earth. He loves us more than our friends or family ever could. His love gives us everything we need.

God will never quit loving you. When you call out to him, he will always respond. At some point, the people around you will disappoint you no matter how much they love you. But God will never disappoint you.

God, your love is greater than anything else in my life.

OCTOBER 1

LOVE AND JOY

> "I have told you these things so that you can have the same joy I have. I want your joy to be the fullest joy."
>
> JOHN 15:11 ICB

Following God's commands is important because God knows what is best for us and he wants us to be joyful. He wants our joy to be the fullest joy! He wants good and wonderful things for his children.

Does following God feel like a chore or a list of things you have to do? If you feel that way, ask God to show you what he wants for you. Ask him to surround you with his love and fill you with joy.

God, thank you for your love that gives me joy.

OCTOBER 2

FOREVER LOVE

Nothing at all can ever separate us from God's love. That's because of what Christ Jesus our Lord has done.

Romans 8:39 nirv

God's love can never be taken away from us. When Jesus died, he made a way for us to be close to God forever. Nothing can change what he did. His sacrifice will last forever.

You are safe and secure in God's love because of Jesus. You don't have to wonder if you are good enough or if God remembers you. His love for you is bigger and stronger than any of your mistakes or problems.

God, thank you for you love that lasts forever.

OCTOBER 3

WILLING AND ABLE

Remember the Lord in everything you do.
And he will give you success.

PROVERBS 3:6 ICB

When we commit our ways to God, he promises to help us. When we put him first, and trust in his plans, he says he will give us success. It is always best to try honor him in all we do.

How can you commit your ways to God? Take time to ask him for help. Remember that he is greater, wiser, and stronger than you are. In everything you do, trust him to guide you.

God, thank you for your wisdom and greatness. I commit my ways to you and trust that you will help me.

OCTOBER 4

IN GOD'S HANDS

There is surely a future hope for you,
and your hope will not be cut off.

PROVERBS 23:18 NIV

God knows each of his children, and he has good plans for all of them. Even when we don't know what our days will look like, we can trust that everything is in God's hands.

God has a wonderful future for you. He will give you the riches of his love whenever you turn to him. There's no way to know the details of future, but you can always put your hope in God's goodness.

God, thank you for holding my future in your hands. Fill me with hope for what's to come.

OCTOBER 5

GOODNESS AND LOVE

> Surely your goodness and love
> will be with me all my life.
> And I will live in the house of the Lord forever.
>
> PSALM 23:6 ICB

We've all had bad days. Sometimes nothing goes the way we want, and it's important to remember the promises God has made. The Bible says that his goodness and love will be with us for our entire lives.

Even when everything goes wrong, you can find comfort in God's goodness and love. God is always with you, and he promises to give you peace.

God, thank you for your goodness and love. Help me remember your promises when life is hard.

OCTOBER 6

THE BODY

> Each of us has one body with many parts. And the parts do not all have the same purpose. So also we are many persons. But in Christ we are one body.
>
> ROMANS 12:4-5 NIRV

Our eyes cannot listen to sounds. Our ears cannot talk, and we can't use our elbows to grasp something we've dropped. Our bodies are made up of different parts, and each part of the body does something special to help us move, grow, and live.

Jesus says that God's family is like a body. Each person does something different. You are one special part of the body, and God doesn't want you to be exactly like any other.

God, thank you for the way you made me. Help me to remember how important it is to just be me!

OCTOBER 7

CHOOSE HUMILITY

> The Lord is pleased with his people.
> He saves those who are not proud.
>
> PSALM 149:4 ICB

Usually, when someone is prideful, they think they know best. Prideful people don't like to accept help, and they don't like to admit when they are wrong. It's hard to save a prideful person because they don't realize they need to be saved in the first place.

God saves those who are not proud. He is close when you need him. Remember who he is and how much you need him. He is always ready to strengthen you when you call upon him.

God, help me to be humble. I don't want to forget how much I need you.

OCTOBER 8

GOOD FRIENDS

Being warned openly is better
than being loved in secret.

PROVERBS 27:5 NIRV

While it's not fun to be corrected, it is good for us. It's better to have friends who are honest than friends who lie just to make us feel better. Ignoring our mistakes might seem nice, but it will cause more problems in the future.

Thank God for the people in your life who are honest. Even though it doesn't always feel good, they are helping you grow. They love you, and they want what is best for you.

God, I want to grow and change each day.

OCTOBER 9

GIFT OF A SMILE

A happy heart makes a face look cheerful.
PROVERBS 15:13 NIRV

When you are having a bad day, a kind face can make a difference. Someone else's happiness can rub off on you when you are feeling sad. It can't solve every problem, but a cheerful smile can be encouraging.

A smile is an easy gift to give. It doesn't cost you anything, and everyone knows what it means. It shows someone you care. Today, see if you can smile at someone who needs it.

God, help me to share joy with others.

OCTOBER 10

ON YOUR SIDE

> What should we say then? Since God is on our side,
> who can be against us?
>
> ROMANS 8:31 NIRV

Every superhero movie has a moment when we realize that the good guy is going to win. We are so confident in their ability that we don't wonder how the movie will end. We know without a doubt, that the hero will win!

Trusting in God is just like that. Nothing is too hard for him. He is on your side, so you have no reason to doubt. God is a strong warrior who fights with you and for you.

God, thank you that you are strong enough to take care of my problems.

OCTOBER 11

DON'T QUIT

"The one who endures to the end will be saved."
MATTHEW 24:13 NLT

Being the first person to cross a finish line feels great! It's so exciting to win. In a race, everyone wants to be first. But our relationship with God is not like a race. We win no matter when we cross the finish line.

Being a Christian is not a competition. It doesn't matter who crosses the finish line first, second, or third. All that matters is that you finish. Your race could be quick and smooth, or it could be slow and full of obstacles. If you don't quit, you win.

God, help me keep my eyes on you.

OCTOBER 12

STRONG AND STEADY

> God always gives you all the grace you need. He will make you strong and steady.
>
> 1 PETER 5:10 NIRV

Some days it seems like everything goes wrong. You stub a toe, lose your homework, trip on the sidewalk, and don't like what is being served for dinner. Sometimes lots of things make you sad. You miss a loved one, a family member gets sick, or your friend doesn't want to talk to you.

Difficult things happen. No matter what, God can give you what you need to get through anything. He always has grace for you. If you ask him, he will make you strong and steady.

God, when I have problems, remind me to come to you.

OCTOBER 13

GOOD CHOICES

Some of you say, "I have the right to do anything." But not everything is helpful.

1 CORINTHIANS 6:12 NIRV

Life is full of choices. We get to decide how we will act and what kind of person we will be. God has given each of us the ability to make good decisions. We can choose to do what honors him, or we can choose to make our own way.

The older you get, the more freedom you will have. Just because you can do something, it doesn't mean you should. Certain activities are not wrong, but they also aren't helpful. Ask God to help you make good choices.

God, I need wisdom to make choices that honor you.

OCTOBER 14

THE BEST NEWS

We are made right with God by putting our faith in Jesus Christ.

ROMANS 3:22 NIRV

God is completely perfect, and our sin gets in the way of us being close to him. This is why we need Jesus. His death on the cross has made us perfect.

Jesus paid a price that you could not. He took the heavy weight of your sin and made you free. When you put your faith in Jesus, you get to be as close to God as you want to!

God, thank you for making me right with you!

OCTOBER 15

EVERY STEP

> "I am very sad I have made Saul king.
> He has not done what I directed him to do."
>
> 1 SAMUEL 15:11 NIRV

Saul was a king in the Bible who stopped listening to God. God had chosen him to be the king, but after a while Saul decided to do everything by himself. Power and riches were more important to Saul than following God's instructions.

Each day you get to choose to obey God. No matter how old you get, it is always best to ask God for his instructions. He is the only one who can keep you on the right path.

God, I want to follow you every day and not go my own way.

OCTOBER 16

YOU ARE SEEN

"You are the God who sees me."

GENESIS 16:13 NIV

God sees us. His attention is always on his children. He is not far away, and we can't hide from him. He also understands us.

When a problem feels like too much for you, you are never alone. Remember that God is with you, and he can give you strength. He is the Creator of the entire universe, and he still sees you.

God, thank you for understanding me and for never leaving me alone.

OCTOBER 17

THE GREAT I AM

"I am who I am. When you go to the people of Israel, tell them, 'I am sent me to you.'"

Exodus 3:14 NCV

In Exodus, we can read about how the Israelites were slaves in Egypt, and God sent Moses to save them. Moses asked God who he should say sent him. This is when God said to tell them, "I am who I am." God is so great he doesn't even have to say his name; people know who he is.

This powerful God is the one you serve. He is on your side. If he can set the slaves free, then he can help you with what you need.

God, thank you for helping me when I need it.

OCTOBER 18

UNDIVIDED ATTENTION

> Teach me your way, Lord,
> that I may rely on your faithfulness;
> give me an undivided heart,
> that I may fear your name.
>
> PSALM 86:11 NIV

It's hard to do two things at once. We can't focus fully on either activity. When our attention is divided between two things, we don't do great at either one. The same is true about following Jesus.

When you focus on Jesus above everything else, your heart will be undivided. When you listen to his voice instead of the voices all around you, you are giving him your full attention. He is more important than anything else in your life.

God, I want to follow you more than anything else.

OCTOBER 19

PRACTICE LISTENING

> Everyone should be quick to listen, slow to speak and slow to become angry.
>
> JAMES 1:19 NIV

We have all spoken too quickly. Sometimes words tumble out of our mouths before we have time to stop ourselves. It's important to learn how to control what we say. When we are good listeners, we make other people feel loved.

It takes practice to be a good listener. It's not something that comes easily to everybody. When you are tempted to speak over someone, remember that what they have to say is just as important as your words.

God, sometimes it's really hard to listen. Teach me how to make others feel noticed and loved.

OCTOBER 20

LOOK FOR HIM

"Everyone who asks will receive. The one who searches will find. And everyone who knocks will have the door opened."

LUKE 11:10 NCV

God is never hiding from us. If we look for him, we will always find him. He promises that he is always available. He is there when we need him, and he will never leave us alone.

No matter what is going on in your life, God is always there. All you have to do is look for him, call out to him, and you will find him.

God, thank you for being easy to find.

OCTOBER 21

TRUE REST

> My health may fail, and my spirit may grow weak,
> but God remains the strength of my heart;
> he is mine forever.
>
> PSALM 73:26 NLT

At the end of the day, we climb into bed and sleep well. We rest, and we wake up refreshed. When our muscles hurt, sleep helps. But what is the solution for a hurting heart?

When your heart is tired or sad, sleep doesn't fix it. God is the one who fixes tired hearts. He is the strength of your heart forever. When you are close to God, he will give you rest and hope that never fades.

God, thank you for giving me true rest.
Help me to come to you when my heart is tired.

OCTOBER 22

TAKE CAPTIVE

We take captive every thought to make it obedient to Christ.

2 CORINTHIANS 10:5 NIV

Just like we can't always control how we feel, we can't always control what we think. Our thoughts are not the most important thing. What matters is what we choose to do with them.

When you think the wrong thing, it is important to recognize it, ask God for forgiveness, and then choose to do the right thing. When you ask him for help, he will show you the right thing to do.

God, when I think something I shouldn't, help me run to you for help.

OCTOBER 23

STRONG WALLS

A person without self-control
is like a city with broken-down walls.

PROVERBS 25:28 NLT

A long time ago, a city would be surrounded by walls to protect it from enemies. If an army were to attack that city, they would have to figure out how to get through the wall. A city with broken walls was not safe from enemies.

Living without self-control is like a city without walls. When you want to hit someone, self-control helps you keep your hands to yourself. When you want to say something mean, self-control helps you keep your mouth shut.

God, thank you for helping me to have self-control.

OCTOBER 24

TAKE NOTICE

> Be joyful with those who are joyful. Be sad with those who are sad.
>
> ROMANS 12:15 NIRV

It's easy to ignore people who are hurting. It's easy to pretend we don't notice someone having a hard time. Sometimes we might even tell ourselves we don't have time to help. This is not what the Bible tells us to do.

God says to be sad with those who are sad even when you don't feel like it. You can help someone feel like they aren't alone just by sitting with them and listening.

God, teach me how to share your love with others especially when they are sad.

PLEASANT AND BEAUTIFUL

> The LORD is all I need.
> He takes care of me.
>
> PSALM 16:5 NCV

God takes care of everything you need, and he is the one who makes something wonderful out of your life.

If you take a moment to think about it, you'll see the ways God has blessed you. He has placed people, things, and memories in your life to bring you joy. Every good gift you have, big or small, is from him.

God, open my eyes and help me see the blessings in my life.

REJOICE

Let the fields and everything in them show their joy.
Then all the trees of the forest will sing for joy.
They will sing before the Lord because he is coming.

PSALM 96:12-13 ICB

We look forward to birthdays, holidays, and special occasions because we know they are good, and we will enjoy them. If we can get excited about a birthday party, imagine the kind of celebration that will happen when Jesus comes back.

When Jesus returns, all of creation will be filled with joy. The Bible says that even the trees will sing. If you are in God's family, you will join in the greatest welcoming party ever!

God, fill me with excitement for when Jesus comes back.

OCTOBER 27

ABOVE ALL ELSE

Teach those who are rich in this world not to be proud and not to trust in their money, which is so unreliable. Their trust should be in God, who richly gives us all we need for our enjoyment.

1 Timothy 6:17 NLT

There are many things that are more important than money. If we put our trust in money, we will eventually be disappointed. Only God can give us riches that will last forever.

You can trust God. He is big enough to take care of everything you need. He is generous with everything he has. Instead of trusting in money or things that make you feel good, put your trust in your heavenly Father.

God, help me to see how important you are.

OCTOBER 28

GOD'S KINGDOM

Better to be patient than powerful;
better to have self-control than to conquer a city.

PROVERBS 16:32 NLT

A lot of things in God's kingdom are the opposite of the world. Those who desire power and control will struggle with being a Christian. God is the one with ultimate power and control.

As you walk with God, you will see it is better to surrender to his greatness than to seek after your own. Praising God, who will be on the throne forever, is the most important thing you can do.

God, protect me from seeking after
my own power and praise.

OCTOBER 29

USE YOUR GIFTS

> The Lord has filled Bezalel with the Spirit of God. The Lord has given Bezalel the skill, ability and knowledge to do all kinds of work. He is able to design pieces to be made of gold, silver and bronze.
>
> EXODUS 35:31-32 ICB

Everybody has been given different gifts. The Bible is full of people like Bezalel who honored God with the gifts he had. It glorifies God when we use our talents and enjoy them.

Your particular gifts or talents might not be obvious to you right now. It's okay to grow into who you are. As you get older, you'll learn what inspires you and how you most like to spend your time.

God, I want to use my gifts to honor you. Show me more about the way you made me.

OCTOBER 30

DELIGHT

> Enjoy serving the LORD,
> and he will give you what you want.
> PSALM 37:4 NCV

It's a lot of fun to give a good gift. It's enjoyable to think about what someone might enjoy, and it's great to see them light up when they open their gift.

If it delights you to give a gift to someone you love, can you imagine how God feels about giving good gifts to you? He is not a genie who will grant all your wishes, but he is the perfect giver, and he loves to bless his children.

God, thank you for the good gifts in my life. You have been so generous and kind to me.

OCTOBER 31

WEAK BUT STRONG

> My goal while I was with you was to talk about only one thing. And that was Jesus Christ and his death on the cross. When I came to you, I was weak and very afraid and trembling all over.
>
> 1 CORINTHIANS 2:2-3 NIRV

Paul, one of the greatest apostles of the New Testament, was afraid to share about Jesus sometimes. It was the power of Jesus that gave him confidence to share the gospel everywhere he went.

Just like Paul, you don't have to worry that you aren't good enough. Jesus' strength is more than enough for you. If you ask him, God will give you courage to share the truth with confidence.

God, thank you for giving me strength when I am weak.

NOVEMBER 1

COLLECTED TEARS

> You have recorded my troubles.
> You have kept a list of my tears.
> Aren't they in your records?
>
> PSALM 56:8 ICB

We don't need to be afraid to come to God with our cares. We can share our deepest feelings. In his presence we will find comfort, hope, compassion, and more love than we can imagine.

God wants to comfort you. He knows how many nights you've had bad dreams, and he collects your tears. He isn't far away when you are sad. He is closer than ever.

God, thank you for caring about me when I am sad.

NOVEMBER 2

HE WILL BE BACK

> He doesn't want anyone to be destroyed. Instead, he wants all people to turn away from their sins.
>
> 2 Peter 3:9 NIrV

If we try to think of everything wrong in the world, we will have a never-ending list. God promised that one day he would fix everything.

Jesus will come back to earth. He promised he would! It might seem like a long time while we are waiting for him to come back, but we still need to believe that he will because he always keeps his promises.

God, thank you for your promises. Help me to remember that one day everything will be perfect.

NOVEMBER 3

TRUE LOVE

> We know what love is because Jesus Christ gave his life for us.
>
> 1 JOHN 3:16 NIRV

Jesus chose to be rejected so that we would be set free. He went through awful pain because he loves us. He laid his life down without complaining. His love and sacrifice are the reason we can be close to God.

You aren't expected to die on a cross, but the Bible says to give your life for your brothers and sisters. This means that you think about what other people need. It means loving and serving others with joy just like Jesus did.

Jesus, thank you for your example of true love.

NOVEMBER 4

BEST DAY EVER

> A single day in your courts
> is better than a thousand anywhere else!
> I would rather be a gatekeeper in the house of my God
> than live the good life in the homes of the wicked.
>
> PSALM 84:10 NLT

God's presence is better than anything else! We all have favorite activities, memories, foods, and people. No matter how wonderful those things might be, God's presence is greater.

The Bible says that just one day in God's house is like your best day ever. Nothing else can compare to the love, peace, and joy that he can give you.

God, I want to spend time with you. Draw me close and give me joy in your presence.

NOVEMBER 5

LIKE JESUS

> Pay everything you owe. But you can never pay back all the love you owe one another. Whoever loves other people has done everything the law requires.
>
> ROMANS 13:8 NIRV

God doesn't have a long list of rules for us to follow. He doesn't make us pay him back or work extra hard when we make mistakes. There is one thing that he thinks we need to do—love others.

It isn't always easy to follow Jesus' example. When you want to hold back your love from others, remember Jesus and his unlimited love.

God, help me to love like Jesus. I want to follow his example and love others no matter what.

NOVEMBER 6

LET GO

> Whoever wants to show love forgives a wrong.
> But those who talk about it separate close friends.
>
> PROVERBS 17:9 NIRV

When someone hurts us, we often want to hold onto that hurt. We want to carry it with us and hold it tight. We might even want to share it with others, so they know how we were wronged.

Sharing every problem you have isn't helpful. It is better to learn how to forgive your friends when they hurt you. It is loving and kind to let something go even when you would rather hold it close.

God, give me wisdom so I know who to talk to when I am hurt.

NOVEMBER 7

PRAISE WITH CREATION

> Let everything that breathes praise the Lord.
> Praise the Lord!
>
> PSALM 150:6 ICB

Sun beams light up the shadows, birds burst into melodies, and trees sway in the breeze as if they are dancing. All of God's creation has ways of praising him, and they all seem to be like a song.

Just like the rest of creation, you bring glory to God by being exactly who he created you to be. He is pleased with you! He is proud that you are his son. Praise him today for all he has done.

God, I lift my praise to you. You are glorious, wonderful, and mighty!

NOVEMBER 8

BE HONEST

The LORD hates those whose lips tell lies.
But he is pleased with people who tell the truth.

PROVERBS 12:22 NIRV

Honesty is always best. Sometimes it's scary to tell the truth, but it is always worth it. When we choose to lie, we break the trust of the people around us. Lying will always lead to problems.

If you lie a lot, people won't believe what you say. That's why it's always best to tell the truth. Ask God to help you tell the truth. He will give you courage and teach you how to be honest.

God, give me strength when I want to lie. Give me an honest heart and a love for the truth.

NOVEMBER 9

JOYFUL TROUBLES

> When troubles of any kind come your way, consider it an opportunity for great joy. For you know that when your faith is tested, your endurance has a chance to grow.
>
> JAMES 1:2-3 NLT

Troubles can bring joy! We don't usually put those two things together, but God does. He says that when problems come up, we can be joyful and strong. He says that when something goes wrong, it helps us grow.

What happens in your head and heart when problems come up? Do you panic or get angry? Do you yell or scream? Ask God to change your heart and he will.

God, I don't always react well to troubles. Give me strength and help me see things the way you do.

NOVEMBER 10

GOD RESTED

> By the seventh day God had finished the work he had been doing; so on the seventh day he rested from all his work.
>
> GENESIS 2:2 ICB

If God chose to rest, we should as well. Even though he is stronger than anyone else, God still said that rest is important. He wants us to work hard, but he also wants us to know how to take a break.

It is good to rest. Your body, heart, and spirit all need breaks. There are so many ways you can rest from your work. Think about a few things that make you feel fresh and alive.

God, give me creative ideas and show me what it looks like to take a break.

NOVEMBER 11

MUCH BETTER

Don't let the world make you impure.

JAMES 1:27 NIRV

God's ways are different from the ways of the world. The world says it's okay to be selfish. The world says the most important things are money, power, and happiness. God says the most important things are loving him and loving others.

If you spend all your time trying to be like the world, your heart will never be satisfied. Instead, go to God and focus on what really matters. Let him love you and share that love with others.

God, you are so much better than the world!

NOVEMBER 12

CONFESS AND HEAL

> Confess your sins to each other and pray for each other so that you may be healed.
>
> JAMES 5:16 NLT

If we don't confess our sins, we won't find healing. It's always better to admit when we are wrong because then we can change and grow.

Be brave and confess your sins. God is gentle and kind. He does not want you to feel guilty, and he is not angry with you. He wants you to be free and full of peace.

God, give me strength to confess my sins. Thank you for healing me when I come to you.

NOVEMBER 13

FEAR THE LORD

> The Lord is pleased with those who fear him,
> with those who trust his love.
>
> PSALM 147:11 ICB

Fearing the Lord means knowing that he is much more powerful than anyone or anything. We are meant to fear the Lord because we know who he is, and we respect him.

Respect for God is a good thing. When you have a healthy fear of God, you will trust that he is able to care for you. You will know that he is strong enough to handle whatever comes your way.

God, teach me how to fear you and trust your love.

NOVEMBER 14

GIVE WHAT YOU HAVE

"This woman is very poor, but she gave all she had."

LUKE 21:4 ICB

Generosity means being willing to share what we have. Generosity is not about how much we have; it's about what is in our hearts. Do we keep everything for ourselves, or do we give no matter what?

God doesn't care how much you have or how much you give. He cares most about your heart. He wants you to be generous if you have a little or if you have a lot.

God, help me to be generous.

NOVEMBER 15

A GOOD FRIEND

Try to understand each other.

1 PETER 3:8 ICB

God made each of us in a unique way, and none of us are completely the same. If we want to love each other well, we must try to understand each other.

God wants you to think about how others feel. When you do this, it makes your friends feel loved. Instead of focusing on how you are different, you can be curious and kind toward people who are different.

God, help me to be kind. I want to be patient and understanding toward the people in my life.

NOVEMBER 16

BAD HABITS

> Let's take a good look at the way we're living.
> Let's return to the Lord.
>
> LAMENTATIONS 3:40 NIRV

We all make mistakes sometimes. We all have things we do that we would like to change. Some of us have a habit of whining when we're asked to do something, while some of us sneak extra cookies after dinner.

What matters most is what you do after your mistakes. Take your messes and give them to God. Ask for forgiveness and repent. Repenting means turning away from your bad habit and acting differently. When you run to God with your mistakes, he is gentle and kind.

God, thank you for your forgiveness.

LOOK OUT FOR DOUBT

> The snake was the most clever of all the wild animals the Lord God had made. One day the snake said to the woman, "Did God really say that you must not eat fruit from any tree in the garden?"
>
> GENESIS 3:1 NCV

One of Satan's best tricks is to make us think we didn't hear what God said. He likes to create doubt. This is how he tempted Eve to eat from the tree of life. She knew what God had told her, but he made her doubt it.

Sometimes, God will tell you something, and it's important to stick to what he says. When you try to come up with reasons not to do it, that is doubting what God has told you.

God, fill my heart with truth. Help me to remember what you've told me to do.

NOVEMBER 18

WORRIES

Give all your worries to him, because he cares about you.

1 Peter 5:7 NCV

When we focus on the negative things in our lives, or the things that might happen, we are filled with worry. Worry can feel stressful. When we focus on what could go wrong, we miss out on the blessings we already have.

God loves to hear what you are worried about, and he loves to take care of you. He is better at it than any person can be.

God, thank you for taking my worries!
Thank you for the strength you give me.

NOVEMBER 19

HANDLING ANGER

> Human anger doesn't produce the holy life God wants.
> So get rid of everything that is sinful.
>
> JAMES 1:20-21 NIRV

Anger never produces goodness. It doesn't solve problems, and it doesn't make us feel better. Anger only produces more anger. It is not wrong to feel angry, but it is wrong to act out in anger.

You can learn to handle your anger in a healthy way. You can try taking deep breaths or counting slowly to ten. You can walk away from the situation and ask for some space. You can go outside and kick a ball around. Talk to God about why you are angry.

God, thank you for being patient with my anger. Teach me how to make good choices when I am upset.

NOVEMBER 20

YOUR SHEPHERD

> He gathers the lambs in his arms
> and carries them close to his heart;
> he gently leads those that have young.
>
> ISAIAH 40:11 NLT

A good shepherd takes care of his lambs. He does everything he can to protect them, and he makes sure they have what they need. He cares for each individual lamb because it is a part of his flock, and every lamb is important.

This is how God sees you. You are like that lamb, and God is like the shepherd. Even though he has an entire flock, he still cares perfectly for you.

God, thank you for being my shepherd. Thank you for taking such good care of me.

NOVEMBER 21

WHATEVER YOU DO

Commit to the Lord whatever you do,
and he will establish your plans.

PROVERBS 16:3 NIV

God wants to be involved in our lives. He wants to guide us through our days, and he wants us to lean on him as we walk through life.

You can commit your homework to him. You can ask him for help with your attitude when you do chores. You can ask him for guidance when you want to be kind to your siblings. When you commit your plans to the Lord, he promises to help you.

God, thank you for helping me
when I commit my plans to you.

NOVEMBER 22

ALL YOUR HEART

"'Love the Lord your God with all your heart, all your soul, and all your mind.' This is the first and most important command."

Matthew 22:37-38 NCV

Being a Christian is more about loving God than doing the right thing. Loving him must come first. When our first priority is to love him with all our heart, mind, and soul, everything else will fall into place.

God cares more about your heart than anything else. As you follow him, he will teach you more about what it means to love him well.

God, I love you! Teach me how to give my whole heart to you.

NOVEMBER 23

GETTING HELP

> The fear of the Lord is the beginning of knowledge,
> but fools despise wisdom and instruction.
>
> PROVERBS 1:7 NIV

The older we get, the more freedom we get. We can do more things on our own. It's good to be able to take care of ourselves, but it's important to know when to ask for help.

Asking for help is wise. God's ways are higher than yours, and he loves to teach his children how to live. When you trust that he knows better than you, you will learn how to love his guidance and correction.

God, thank you for being bigger and smarter than I am.

NOVEMBER 24

EVEN MORE

> "You believe because you see me. Those who believe without seeing me will be truly happy."
>
> JOHN 20:29 ICB

The disciples walked with Jesus and got to see miracles with their own eyes. They could hear his voice, ask him questions, and see his face when he spoke.

The Bible says that because you have followed Jesus with just the faith in your heart, you will be rewarded even more. God knows how hard it is to have faith in something you cannot see, and he is very proud of you.

God, fill my heart with truth and keep me close to you.

NOVEMBER 25

GOD KNOWS

> Everything a person does might seem pure to them.
> But the Lord knows why they do what they do.
>
> PROVERBS 16:2 NIRV

It's really easy to make judgments about why other people act the way they do. It's easy to think we have the answers to every situation. The truth is only God can see into the hearts of people.

When you make assumptions, you take the other person's voice away from them. Instead, try asking questions. Ask God to help you see others the way he sees them.

God, help me to see others the way you do.

NOVEMBER 26

ANSWERS

> Now I know only a part. But at that time I will know fully, as God has known me.
>
> 1 CORINTHIANS 13:12 ICB

No matter how old we get, there will always be things we don't understand. Not everything has an explanation. Until we are face-to-face with Jesus, our knowledge will not be complete.

God has promised to give you full understanding when Jesus comes back. Then, everything will make sense. You can always trust that God is in control.

God, help me to trust you when I am unsure.

NOVEMBER 27

BE PREPARED

> The time is near when all things will end. So think clearly and control yourselves so you will be able to pray.
>
> 1 Peter 4:7 NCV

When guests come over, we usually spend some time getting ready. We might tidy up our house or make something to eat. We want our company to feel at home, so we do our best to prepare for them.

Just like your family might prepare for a guest to visit, you can prepare for Jesus. The day is coming when he will return. While you wait for him, do your best to honor him with the way you live.

God, help me to prepare for Christ's return. Show me how I can honor you with all my days.

NOVEMBER 28

A DIFFERENT STANDARD

> God's grace has been given to me. So here is what I say to every one of you. Don't think of yourself more highly than you should.
>
> ROMANS 12:3 NIRV

When we only think about ourselves, we are being self-centered. God has called us to a different standard. He said it is more important to think about others. We shouldn't assume that we are the best.

It takes faith to be considerate of others because you have to trust that God will take care of you. When you believe he will provide for you, can put others' needs before your own.

God, forgive me for the times I have been self-centered. Give me grace to put others first.

NEEDED

> Some parts of the body that seem weakest and least important are actually the most necessary. So, God has put the body together such that extra honor and care are given to those parts that have less dignity.
>
> 1 Corinthians 12:24 NLT

The body of Christ is like a puzzle. Each person is like a puzzle piece, and we are all connected to make something wonderful. Without one piece, the picture would not be complete.

You are an important part of the body of Christ. You have a specific role to play, and God is proud of you. As you get older, you will learn more about the role you play in the body of Christ.

God, show me where I fit in the body of Christ. Help me to grow into the man you created me to be.

NOVEMBER 30

LEARN TO LIVE

> Do not be shaped by this world. Instead be changed within by a new way of thinking. Then you will be able to decide what God wants for you. And you will be able to know what is good and pleasing to God and what is perfect.
>
> ROMANS 12:2 ICB

We get to choose how we will live and how we will be shaped. We can let the world influence us, or we can learn how God wants us to live. The more we look for his ideas, the more we will know what is right.

As a follower of Jesus, there will be times in your life when you are tempted to live in a way that doesn't honor God. The more you walk with God, the more you will learn to think the way he thinks.

God, show me what is good and pleasing to you.

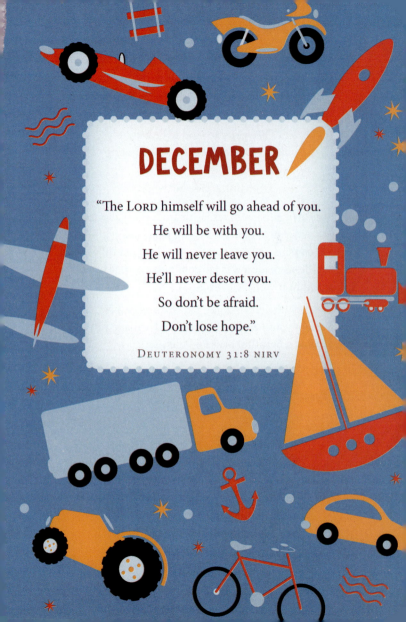

DECEMBER

"The Lord himself will go ahead of you.
He will be with you.
He will never leave you.
He'll never desert you.
So don't be afraid.
Don't lose hope."

Deuteronomy 31:8 nirv

DECEMBER 1

THE GIFT OF PEACE

"Give glory to God in heaven,
and on earth let there be peace among
the people who please God."

LUKE 2:14 NCV

Jesus was on a mission to rescue us from every thought, word, or action that didn't match up with God's goodness. He took our sins with him on the cross and got rid of them for good. Jesus made a way for goodness to come back into the human heart.

God's peace is the greatest gift you will ever receive. God doesn't want your heart to be troubled. He made you, loves you, and has a beautiful plan for your life.

God, thank you for the gift of peace.

DECEMBER 2

SATISFIED

I will be content as if I had eaten the best foods.
My lips will sing. My mouth will praise you.

PSALM 63:5 ICB

God's love is better than life! Knowing, loving, and following him is better than anything else. We will be the happiest when we are with him.

When you praise God, he fills your heart with peace. When you spend time with him, he surrounds you with love. When you surrender to his plans, he gives you grace to get through each day.

God, your love is better than anything else in life.

DECEMBER 3

WATER OF LIFE

> "Anyone who drinks the water I give them will never be thirsty. In fact, the water I give them will become a spring of water in them. It will flow up into eternal life."
>
> JOHN 4:14 NIRV

Wouldn't it be amazing to never feel hungry or thirsty? We wouldn't get a headache because we forgot to drink water, or ever have to wait for dinner to be ready. It's hard to even imagine a life without needing to eat or drink.

Jesus says that loving him is like never being thirsty again. He means that loving him will satisfy your heart forever. Jesus says that he will always be there for us, like a big bottle of water that never runs out.

Jesus, thank you for giving me eternal life. You are the fountain that never runs dry!

DECEMBER 4

GOODNESS AND LIGHT

> You are the giver of life.
> Your light lets us enjoy life.
>
> PSALM 36:9 ICB

God is the giver of life. He created each one of us, and he knows what is best for us. He is a perfect father who knows exactly what each of his children need. Life is enjoyable because of the light he gives us.

Every good thing in your life is from God. No matter what anyone else says, you can't truly know goodness without knowing him.

God, I want to live in your light! Thank you for filling my life with your goodness.

DECEMBER 5

EVERY DAY

> Just as you received Christ Jesus as Lord, continue to live your lives in him.
>
> COLOSSIANS 2:6 NIV

It's important to know how to work at something each day. We can't snap our fingers and expect a job to be done. We must follow the steps that are needed without giving up.

The same is true about your relationship with Jesus. The day that you accepted Jesus into your life was so important. It's equally important to keep loving Jesus every day of your life. Following him is not a one-time decision.

Jesus, help me to remember to keep you in my mind and my heart each day.

DECEMBER 6

SAY YES

> The yes to all of God's promises is in Christ, and through Christ we say yes to the glory of God.
>
> 2 CORINTHIANS 1:20 NCV

Jesus is God's biggest yes! God made a lot of good promises. He said that we would be forgiven, be part of his family, and have eternal life. All of these things are possible because of Jesus.

When you say yes to Jesus, you are accepting all of God's best promises. There is no other way of living that is better than following Jesus. In him, you will always have what you need.

God, I say yes to your promises for my life.

DECEMBER 7

SHARPEN AND IMPROVE

As iron sharpens iron,
so people can improve each other.

PROVERBS 27:17 NCV

As followers of God, we can make each other better. We can encourage each other and lift each other up. We can take turns being strong. We are a team, a body, and a family. We need each other.

You get to decide who your friends are. Do your best to surround yourself with people who make you better. Ask God to give you friends who sharpen you.

God, help me make good choices with my friends.

DECEMBER 8

NEVER ALONE

> "Teach them to obey everything that I have taught you, and I will be with you always, even until the end of this age."
>
> MATTHEW 28:20 NCV

A lot of people don't like to be alone. The good news is that Jesus promises he will always be with us. When we follow Jesus, we are never alone. He knows exactly what our lives look like, and he is with us every step of the way.

When you feel lost, remember Jesus is with you. When you feel sad, confused, or frustrated, remember Jesus is with you. You don't have to deal with your emotions alone, and you don't have to figure out your life on your own.

Jesus, thank you for always being with me.

DECEMBER 9

PRAISE HELPS

I will praise the LORD at all times;
his praise is always on my lips.

PSALM 34:1-2 NCV

For each problem, there is a solution. When we are tired, we rest. When we are hungry, we eat. When there is a problem in our heart, we can talk to God about it.

When you praise God, your heart feels better. You can go from mad to peaceful, or from afraid to brave. There is always a reason to thank God. Look for things to thank him for.

God, thank you for changing my heart when I praise you.

DECEMBER 10

STRONG AND BRAVE

"I was with Moses, so I will be with you.
I will not leave you or forget you.
Joshua, be strong and brave!"

JOSHUA 1:5-6 NCV

God asked Moses to do brave things like leave his home, talk to an angry leader, and perform miracles. Moses was afraid, but God promised to be with him. Then he promised he would be with Joshua when he asked Joshua to do brave things.

God will be with you too! Even if something seems wild and scary, you can trust God. He will give you what you need.

God, help me be brave and do what you ask.
Thank you for always being with me!

DECEMBER 11

GOD NOTICES

> He is a father to orphans, and he defends the widows.
> God gives the lonely a home.
>
> PSALM 68:5-6 NCV

A good dad notices when one of his children is sad. He pays attention to their cries, and he does his best to fix the problem. He keeps his children safe, and he provides a home for them.

God is the best dad. He is your heavenly Father, and he loves to take care of you. Even when no one notices that you need something, God knows. He is always there when you need him.

God, thank you for taking good care of me. Thank you for being the best dad ever!

A LONG TIME

He chose us before the world was made so that we would be his holy people.

Ephesians 1:4 NCV

You may have noticed that as people get older, they don't remember as much. As time goes by our memories get worse, but God knows and remembers everything.

God chose you to be his before the world was even made. All of history is clear in his mind, and nothing is hidden from him. He is not limited by time the way you are. You, and all of creation, are safe in his hands.

God, thank you for loving me even before the world began.

DECEMBER 13

WISDOM

Learn the truth and never reject it.
Get wisdom, self-control, and understanding.

PROVERBS 23:23 NCV

Wisdom is knowing what is right and then doing it. When we want to lie, it takes wisdom to tell the truth. When we want to yell or hit someone, it takes wisdom to walk away.

If you need wisdom, God will give it to you. He promises to give wisdom to whoever asks. He will give you a never-ending supply of wisdom if you seek him for it.

God, give me wisdom so I can
make choices that honor you.

DECEMBER 14

EXPECTATIONS

> Teach me to do your will,
> for you are my God.
> May your gracious Spirit lead me forward
> on a firm footing.
>
> PSALM 143:10 NLT

We can put a lot of pressure on ourselves. We think we should have certain things figured out, and we feel bad about ourselves when we fail. We want to do our best at everything, but sometimes we just don't know what we are doing.

God does not expect you to know everything. He doesn't want you to have all the answers, and he doesn't think you should do everything right the first time. He only wants you to go to him and let him lead you.

God, I trust you to lead me.

DECEMBER 15

GOD IS LOVE

We know the love that God has for us, and we trust that love. God is love.

1 JOHN 4:16 NCV

We can't see God, but we know he loves us. The Bible is clear that God's love for us will last forever, and we can trust that it will not fail. There will never be a time when God's love isn't available.

You can't know God without knowing his love. Everything about him is loving. You could spend your whole life learning more and more about it, and you wouldn't have enough days.

God, thank you for your love. Give me a greater understanding of how much you love me.

DECEMBER 16

WHEN JESUS RETURNS

> If we look forward to something we don't yet have, we must wait patiently and confidently.
>
> ROMANS 8:25 NLT

This part of the Bible is talking about waiting for Jesus to come back a second time. After he died on the cross and rose again, Jesus said that he would return and make everything right again. We wait for him patiently and confidently because we know he will do what he says.

On really hard days, you can put your hope in Jesus' return. No troubles will last forever because when he returns, everything will be perfect.

Jesus, help me to wait patiently and confidently for your return.

DECEMBER 17

TRUSTWORTHY

> The Lord is trustworthy in all he promises
> and faithful in all he does.
>
> PSALM 145:13 NIV

God is trustworthy and faithful. This means you can depend on him. It means that he never quits, and he is steady. God will never get tired or change his mind about loving you. He always keeps his promises.

When you know that God is trustworthy and faithful, you can have confidence in who he is and how he sees you.

God, thank you for being trustworthy and faithful! Give me confidence in who you are.

DECEMBER 18

POINTING FINGERS

> Make allowances for each other's faults, and forgive anyone who offends you. Remember, the Lord forgave you, so you must forgive others.
>
> COLOSSIANS 3:13 NIV

No one is perfect. We all make mistakes. This is important to remember when the people around us do the wrong thing. We are not better than they are. It might seem easy to point fingers, but this is not how God asks us to treat each other.

God asks you to forgive others for their mistakes just like he has forgiven you. If you ask, God will soften your heart and give you grace to forgive.

God, thank you for forgiving my sins. Help me to forgive others in the same way.

DECEMBER 19

GIFT GIVER

A secret gift will calm an angry person.
PROVERBS 21:14 NCV

A little kindness goes a long way. When we are sad, tired, or angry, a gift can make all the difference. It makes us feel loved when someone takes the time to do something kind for us.

Finding a secret gift is wonderful! It's also wonderful to practice being a giver of secret gifts. You can bless other people by leaving them a note or a thoughtful present.

God, show me opportunities to encourage others by giving gifts.

DECEMBER 20

GOD GIVES HOPE

> I pray that the God who gives hope will fill you with much joy and peace while you trust in him.
>
> ROMANS 15:13 NCV

Feeling hopeless is like feeling stuck or trapped. We might feel hopeless about a certain subject at school, thinking we'll never understand it. We might feel hopeless during a week that is so rainy it feels like the sun will never come out again. Hopelessness is a horrible feeling.

God can fill you with hope. If you are ever in a situation where you don't have hope, God says he can fix it. As you tell him about your problem, he will give you joy and peace.

God, thank you for being the giver of hope.

DECEMBER 21

GROWING LOVE

> We ought always to thank God for you, brothers and sisters, and rightly so, because your faith is growing more and more, and the love all of you have for one another is increasing.
>
> 2 THESSALONIANS 1:3 NIV

As we grow in faith, our love for others will also grow. As we follow Jesus and understand more about him, we learn to love as he did. He loved the people no one else loved. He noticed people who had been ignored. This is the kind of love that we are supposed to have for others.

You don't get to decide if someone deserves to be loved. God says to love everyone in the same way you love yourself.

God, thank you for teaching me how to love others like you love me.

DECEMBER 22

BETTER THAN MONEY

> Don't wear yourself out trying to get rich.
> Wealth can vanish in the wink of an eye.
>
> PROVERBS 23:4-5 NCV

When we are young, money seems really exciting. Every dollar we earn is like more freedom to get the next thing we want. Money is not the most important thing in life.

Loving others and honoring God are more important than money. The Bible says not to wear yourself out trying to get rich. Instead, give your time and energy to things that will last.

God, teach me how to love you and others more than I love money.

DECEMBER 23

PURPOSE

> In Christ we were chosen to be God's people. God had already chosen us to be his people, because that is what he wanted. And God is the One who makes everything agree with what he decides and wants.
>
> EPHESIANS 1:11 ICB

When we are young, it's fun to dream about the future. We might wonder what kind of person we will be, where we will live, or what our family will look like. We imagine the career we will have and the adventures we will go on.

It is great to imagine what kind of life you will live. God has given you wonderful dreams, but no matter what you do, your most important purpose is to glorify God.

God, help me to remember I am your son before anything else.

DECEMBER 24

STEADY AND SAFE

"I am the resurrection and the life. Anyone who believes in me will live, even if they die. And whoever lives by believing in me will never die. Do you believe this?"

JOHN 11:25-26 NIRV

We all have doubts sometimes. No matter what age we are, we sometimes feel unsure about our relationship with God. It's not bad to have doubts, but it is important what you choose to do with those thoughts.

When doubt creeps into your mind, turn to what the Bible says. Jesus says that he is the reason you are saved, not because of anything you have done. You are safe in Jesus hands even when you don't feel like it.

God, when I have doubts, remind me to depend on what's true.

DECEMBER 25

GOOD NEWS

The shepherds went quickly and found Mary and Joseph. And the shepherds saw the baby lying in a feeding box. Then they told what the angels had said about this child. Everyone was amazed when they heard what the shepherds said to them.

LUKE 2:16-18 ICB

When the shepherds were told about Jesus, they ran as fast as their feet could carry them! They rushed to Bethlehem and into the barn to see him. After they had seen the baby, they knew he was the Savior of the world, and they went to tell everyone about him.

Hallelujah! Christ has come! Tell your friends. Tell your neighbors. Tell everyone you meet—Jesus is the Lord, and he has come to give us life.

Jesus, thank you for coming to give the whole world new life.

DECEMBER 26

TELL THE TRUTH

> Stop telling lies. Let us tell our neighbors the truth, for we are all parts of the same body.
>
> EPHESIANS 4:25 NLT

Telling the truth is important because it has an effect on the people around us. When we lie, it causes damage to our relationships.

Lying creates a space where trust cannot live. Be someone who tells the truth because you love others. When you speak words that are real and true, you show you care.

God, help me to be honest even when it's hard.

DECEMBER 27

CAREFUL WORDS

> Let the words you speak always be full of grace. Learn how to make your words what people want to hear. Then you will know how to answer everyone.
>
> COLOSSIANS 4:6 NIRV

Words are powerful. We are each responsible for what comes out of our mouths. As followers of Jesus, we should try our best to be careful with our words.

What you say is important. Being polite and kind can change someone's day for the better. It can be tempting to try to sound cool with your words. Instead, let the things you say be encouraging and mindful.

God, teach me how to be careful with my words.

DECEMBER 28

LOVE OVER FEAR

There is no fear in love. Instead, perfect love drives away fear. That's because fear has to do with being punished. The one who fears does not have perfect love. We love because he loved us first.

1 JOHN 4:18-19 NIRV

If we follow God only because we don't want to be punished, fear will grow in our hearts. If we are afraid of God, we will not follow him for long. Fear does not last, and fear does not make us strong. Only love can make us strong.

God does not want to punish you. He does not want you to be ashamed or embarrassed. He wants you to have peace and lightness in your heart. God wants his love to set you free.

God, fill my heart with your love! Take my fear and help me see how kind you are.

DECEMBER 29

WORTHLESS

All things are worth nothing compared with the greatness of knowing Christ Jesus my Lord. Because of him, I have lost all those things, and now I know they are worthless trash. This allows me to have Christ.

Philippians 3:8 NCV

Jesus is our greatest treasure. The world and all of its riches cannot compare to knowing him. When we spend all of our time searching for what makes us feel good, we miss out on the delight of knowing Christ.

Be careful not to get caught up in the desire for more and more stuff. Instead, ask God to show you the goodness that is found in Jesus.

God, thank you for the goodness of knowing Jesus.

DECEMBER 30

NOTHING ELSE

> Some trust in chariots.
> Some trust in horses.
> But we trust in the LORD our God.
>
> PSALM 20:7 NIRV

There is no amount of wealth or power that can protect us like God can. He is the true king of the entire universe. He is the one who knows everything, sees everything, and holds everything safely in his hands.

Dare to trust in God. Something you need might seem impossible, but that doesn't mean God can't manage it. He created the world! Take all of your wild and impossible dreams and put them in God's hands.

God, you are mighty, strong, and glorious! I don't want to trust in anyone more than I trust in you.

DECEMBER 31

FULLY EQUIPPED

"You have a large number of skilled stonemasons and carpenters and craftsmen of every kind. You have expert goldsmiths and silversmiths and workers of bronze and iron. Now begin the work, and may the Lord be with you!"

1 Chronicles 22:15-16 NLT

God told his people to build the temple. He didn't give them the job and then leave them alone to figure it out. He made sure they had the instructions, tools, and workers that were needed.

God will do the same thing for you. He doesn't ask you to do a job and then leave you alone. If he has told you to do something, he will make sure you have what you need to do it well.

God, help me to remember you have given me everything I need to do what you ask me to.